TOMMY HEINSOHN TELLS IT AS HE SEES IT . . .

ON BILL RUSSELL:
"Here was Russell, this big, skinny black kid whom cops in San Francisco used to pick up and stick into lineups whever they were doing sweeps just because he was black. He was a winner, but he sure wasn't an affable guy. He was suspicious of new relationships, especially with whites, and now he had come to a city not known for its hospitality to blacks."

ON THE '56–'64 CELTICS:
"Were we the best team ever? I don't know. I'd say eight championships in a row certainly makes a compelling case. . . . I'll tell you this: We were the hardest team of all time to beat."

ON EX-KNICKS COACH HUBIE BROWN:
"A loser in Atlanta before he became a bigger loser in New York . . . an elitist who thought ex-players knew nothing. . . ."

GIVE 'EM THE HOOK

"A TOTALLY HONEST STORY . . . WHICH SHOULD BE READ BY ANYONE HOOKED ON SPORTS—FOR THE FUN OF IT, AND FOR THE GOOD OF IT."
—Bobby Orr,
Boston Bruins Hall of Famer

"TAKE IT FRO~~M~~ . . . ~~TH~~IS BOOK IS GRE~~AT~~ . . . A WINNER."—~~"T~~

For~~mer~~ . . . ~~execu~~tives

GIVE 'EM THE HOOK

TOMMY HEINSOHN
AND JOE FITZGERALD

POCKET BOOKS

New York   London   Toronto   Sydney   Tokyo   Singapore

POCKET BOOKS, a division of Simon & Schuster
1230 Avenue of the Americas, New York, NY 10020

ISBN: 0-671-73268-4

First Pocket Books printing February 1991

10 9 8 7 6 5 4 3 2 1

POCKET and colophon are registered trademarks of
Simon & Schuster.

Printed in the U.S.A.

To those who cared
when it mattered most

○ Acknowledgments ○

A book, like a basketball team, is a singular reflection of collective efforts, not all of which receive their proper due. The authors, beneficiaries of such contributions, would like to express their warmest gratitude to the following: Thomas Boylston Adams, Ross Atkin, John Cronin, Mike Globetti, Ed Hobart, Navy Labnon, Richard Lord, Heidi McGuigan, Jeff Twiss, Jan Volk, and Arlys Warfield.

We would also like to offer special thanks to: John Hinchey, whose technical support was invaluable and whose personal support was incalculable; Bob Sales, whose creative juices added to the flow, but who also helped in ways even he doesn't know; Larry Moulter, our agent, who had the vision before anyone and then brought it into focus for everyone; and, finally, Paul Aron, our editor, who was always there when we needed guidance and yet never intruded on the time we needed to be alone.

We are indebted to them all.

○ Contents ○

Contents

Contents

Contents

Contents

◦ **1** ◦

The Neighborhood Nazi

There are moments that stay with you forever; and if your life has been caught up in sports the way my life has been, then there are games that stay with you forever, too.

I've had more than my share of moments, especially during those nine seasons I played with the Celtics, when we won eight championships. But the one that means the most to me today, the one that pleases me for reasons no one else may understand, occurred in 1974, my fifth year as coach of the Celts, when I came as close as I'm ever apt to come to stepping inside the mind and the spirit of a lifelong hero of mine.

That was the day, in *my* mind, that I thought I knew what it felt like to be Vincent van Gogh.

I can remember thinking about him that morning as we got ready to play the Bucks in Game 7 for the title, which, if we won it, would be my first as coach and Boston's first since the end of the Bill Russell dynasty in 1969.

We'd come very close to sewing it up on our own

court two nights earlier when John Havlicek sent a rainbow shot over the outstretched arms of Kareem Abdul-Jabbar to give us a 101–100 lead with seven seconds to go in double overtime. Things looked so good, in fact, that Garden fans were already partying in the aisles when Kareem answered back, taking an inbounds pass in front of our bench, dribbling twice, then releasing one of those soft sky hooks that hit nothing but net as it fell through the hole.

Final score: Milwaukee 102, Boston 101.

That's a tough way to lose. Now, instead of celebrating what we'd worked so hard to attain, instead of being rewarded for the way we'd busted our buns that entire series with the most aggressive type of defense you could ask of a team at that time of the season, we were forced to go home, pack our bags, and go on the road again, this time for a game no one really believed we could win.

I told the players to put it out of their minds for the night, to get whatever sleep they could, that we'd talk about it again in the morning. Then I headed downstairs to my office with John Killilea, my assistant, and Bob Cousy, my old teammate, and the three of us huddled into the wee hours, reviewing my whole philosophy of guarding Kareem. The standard way of doing it, the accepted way throughout the league, was to double-team him, but we never did it that way. It was always my belief that the one weakness he might have was stamina, so we attacked his stamina—the way we did with Bob Lanier and Willis Reed—by having Dave Cowens hound him all over the floor, challenging him one-on-one, while making sure our defense shut down everyone else.

That was our stated philosophy and everyone knew it, including Larry Costello, the Milwaukee coach. But now here we were, tied at 3–3 with one game to go for all the marbles. I remember telling Cooz I thought the time was right for a change of strategy, not because I didn't believe in what we were doing, but because they wouldn't expect it, and we needed to catch them by surprise, to gain some kind of quick first-quarter advantage that might knock them off their pins. That's what you always hope to do when you're going on the road for that final game.

The politically expedient thing to have done was nothing. They were odds-on favorites to beat us out there. We were the smallest team in the league, the clear underdogs; we would have had legitimate reasons for losing. The change I was proposing—having Paul Silas, our power forward, leave his man, Cornell Warner, and double up on Kareem—wasn't all that radical, but the timing was radical. I knew if it didn't work I'd be laying my job on the line. With the gathering of the storm, certain members of the media would be sure to ask: "How could he expect to change his defense in one day and still win the flag?" There was no question in my mind that I'd be leaving myself wide open to that kind of criticism.

Nevertheless, that was the decision we arrived at in my office that night, and the next day I proposed it to the players. "Guys," I said, "it's very simple. This has now become Cornell Warner's championship to win or to lose. We're going to dare him to be a great player tomorrow. If he is, if he hits those shots we're going to give him, they win the championship. If he misses, we do."

Warner played 29 minutes and scored 1 point. Meanwhile, we held Kareem scoreless for almost 18 minutes, from the end of the first quarter until 5:33 of the third, as we built up a 17-point lead, 63–46. By then the game was, in effect, over. We just coasted from there to a final winning margin of 102–87.

That decision, to me, has come to represent me as a person and a coach. I took great pride in it, and not just because I thought it was poker playing at its best. What pleased me most as I savored it on the flight home was the fact that I hadn't done the political thing, which was to play it safe. I *dared* to win and, as a result, we flew home with the pot.

When you do things like that—when, in essence, you gamble to win and expose yourself to failure— what you're really doing is testing yourself as a person; you're taking all that you are—your personality, your intelligence, your emotions, your security—and you're testing that against what you believe is the correct way to proceed to the next step. You don't know if you're right or wrong—it's a calculated judgment—but if the element of risk wasn't in the equation, it wouldn't be a test at all. It's that willingness to be different, to be an individual, to sink or swim with your own decisions, that's always fascinated me.

Knute Rockne, for one, exemplified that when he inaugurated a shifting backfield at Notre Dame on an inspiration he got while watching chorus girls dance at a show in Chicago. He took something totally irrelevant to football and found in it a concept that could broaden the possibilities of what he was doing as a coach. He saw something in that movement he thought would confuse defensive alignments.

He could have been laughed at. He could have been ridiculed. Can you imagine the field day newspapers would have had if his hunch had been wrong? COACH TURNS FIGHTING IRISH INTO DANCING GIRLS ROUTINE! Yet he was willing to act on his beliefs and to act at the proper time, when his beliefs would have their greatest impact. He saw something nobody had thought of before, something he thought would give his team an edge over a period of time, and he made his move.

I love to see that in people. It seems to me we see less and less of it as time goes by.

Of course what I did that afternoon in Milwaukee was not unusual; other teams played Kareem the same way throughout the regular season. But the

Celtics didn't. Everyone knew our philosophy was to play him one up, to make him be great every night. All I did was recognize a scenario the Bucks never would've expected, so it was more of a sneak attack, a flanking movement, than anything else. Still, it carried the obvious risk of failure, which was what made the ultimate success so satisfying.

The real geniuses in anything—art, sport, what have you—are, I think, the ones who fly in the face of accepted mores, who push whatever it is they do beyond the current understanding, who go past what their peers can understand. It's as if they have an innate light that penetrates the darkness, and it's only these explorers of the unknown who really extend the boundaries of anything. Somehow or other, this light enables them to open up the blackness of the future and allows them to see exciting new vistas. Their passion is consuming, always drawing them to new directions.

That was Rockne.

For one afternoon in Milwaukee, I almost felt it was me.

In essence, that was the story of Vincent van Gogh. That's why I've always admired him. I liked his strength of character. He had an itch to be an artist, indeed a compulsive desire to be one, so he slaved at his paintings all of his life, never selling one and never receiving even a moment's worth of reinforcement that he had any talent at all. It would be years after his death before the world finally recognized his genius. But he wasn't painting for the masses; he was painting for *himself*. So he persevered and followed his own light through all kinds of frustrations, including a mental condition, because he was convinced that he was on the right track, or at least the track that seemed right for him.

Boy, is *that* a vanishing quality.

* * *

I began reading about van Gogh a long time ago, when I first got involved in art. I guess what his life story has always said to me is that if you're going to be worth anything, if you're really going to be good at what you do, you have to believe in yourself and in what you're doing and not be subject to the whims of other people. Oh, you can listen to what they have to say, but ultimately it's *you* who has to make the decisions.

When I talk with kids today, I ask them the same thing I asked my own kids as they were growing up: "What do you want to be? Do you want to be an individual, or do you just want to be one of the boys?" You see, if you want to be special, then you can't be worrying about what other people might think, even if it means being ostracized. If you want to play a piano or a violin, rather than whatever the *in* instrument happens to be, for whatever pleasure it accords you, whatever fulfillment you get from it, you've got to be able to withstand peer pressure. You've got to make a conscious decision that you won't allow others to deter you from whatever it is that might make you distinct.

That willingness, that ability to stand apart from the crowd, is not easy to come by; it never has been. But it's always been important, and for kids today it's probably more important than ever because with the choices facing young people now, the wrong decision can kill you.

I was forced to learn that early. I didn't worry about my peer group because, for a long time, I didn't have a peer group.

I grew up in Jersey City, New Jersey, in what would properly be described as a tough, working-class neighborhood. It wasn't abject poverty or anything like that; but still, my father lost his job during the Depression and, like a lot of other families, we were trying to put it all together when World War II came along.

6

I was seven when the Japanese attacked Pearl Harbor in 1941, drawing us into the battle; and for me the war came home in a very personal, distressing manner. Being the only German kid in the neighborhood, I was quickly singled out as the resident "Nazi," which meant having to fight my way home from school nearly every day. The O'Briens, Perullis, and DePintos would all be waiting when school got out; waiting to knock me down, to jump on top of me, to begin throwing punches all at once, kicking me and calling me names. It was one kid against four or five all the time, sometimes one against all three families at once.

We entered the war in December and this stuff began happening in January. Every day it went on; every day I was forced to run this gauntlet home from grammar school. I began taking different routes, sometimes going seven or eight blocks out of my way and then climbing over the back fence to get into my house without having to confront ten or twelve guys who wanted to whip my ass. Let me assure you, that's a bitch for a young kid. When they realized I had eluded them they'd come up onto our porch and start banging on the windows, taunting me, calling me everything they could think of; and there I was, inside, alone, hearing it all and not daring to step out into that kind of an atmosphere. It was devastating; that's the only word for it. It was also very lonely, a loneliness tinged with terror.

If all this had happened when I was ten or eleven I might have gone outside and punched a few faces. Instead, it came at a crucial point in my development and really rocked me around, even to the point of my developing neuroses that are still with me today, neuroses I'm learning to deal with even now.

My father was a big man, a foreman in a warehouse. He loved to swim, and he was in such great shape that when he lost his job at age fifty-five he was able to get another one by passing himself off as forty-three. So his answer to my predicament was to get physical, to confront the challenge head-on. Whenever he heard my tormentors near the house he'd take me outside and tell them, "Listen, this kid's not afraid of any of you, and he's going to fight one of you right *now!* You pick out your best guy and he'll fight him right here, one-on-one." And that's what I'd do. I'd be crying like a sucker; but, man, I'd also be getting my whacks in at one of those guys, trying to get even, trying to make him pay for what the group of them had done to me. It would be my only chance to do it without having to fight them all at once, so I'd try to make the most of it. Scared? Oh yeah, I'd be scared all right. But I'd be furious, too, and with my father urging me on I'd more than hold my own, which meant, for the time being at least, I gained some measure of respect.

My mother, of course, would get very upset with my father whenever he'd do this, but he'd always tell her, "Hey, the kid did all right!" He'd feel good about it and so would I. That's the way my father taught me to solve my problems. Be aggressive. Be competitive. And I think his influence was evident throughout my playing career. I came to believe that the first way to gain acceptance and dignity was to get it in a physical way—"Hey, there goes the leading scorer of the high school team!"—and it became very important to me to be recognized like that, because of all the ego damage that had come from being the neighborhood Nazi in the second grade.

Still, the relief was only temporary. The neighborhood kids would leave me alone for a day or two, but then the abuse would start up again and I'd be back inside the house, alone, listening to them banging on the windows, daring me to fight without my father looking on, telling me what a loathsome person I was. That was quite a load for someone seven years old.

8

There were many times I sat there crying, wondering to myself: *Why are they so mad at me? I'm no Nazi. I'm living in the United States!*

But that's what was going on in my life; so, out of necessity, I learned early to be a loner. I learned to operate *without* a peer group. I learned I didn't have to play with other kids all of the time in order to enjoy myself. And I learned something else from that experience, something very valuable. I learned that some people are going to like you, no matter what, and some people are going to hate you, no matter what, and there's probably nothing you can do to change their minds. That's why making it into the Hall of Fame—though I was pleased to be inducted in 1986—was almost immaterial to me. I learned a long time ago that the ultimate thing is to satisfy yourself, to accept a challenge, to master something, whatever it is, because of what it means to you, and not to measure it by what it might mean to other people. You have no control over that.

While other kids my age were looking for approbation and group acceptance—"Let's *all* go swimming! Let's *all* do this together! Let's *all* do that together!"—I learned to entertain myself. I had to; there was no such thing as television back in those days. You listened to "Jack Armstrong" on the radio and that was about it. So I learned how to be alone, and while it wasn't pleasant and certainly wasn't what I'd have chosen, I came to accept it after a while, and at times 1 even enjoyed it.

I created a world of my own in which painting became my friend. I started drawing as a way to amuse myself, and in time I became fairly proficient at it. I'd show my drawings to my mother but not to anyone else, because, like van Gogh, I wasn't drawing for anyone else; I was drawing for myself.

Yet she was forever concerned about all the time I spent alone. So she'd arrange for me to go to someone's house once a week after school, just so I'd occasionally have someone to play with. And she was always trying to get me to join Cub Scouts, Boy Scouts, *anything* that would expand my very limited social horizon. None of that really appealed to me, however, so I continued to draw and stay pretty much by myself until, a few years later, I came upon a new friend, a friend I hit it off with right away, a friend who provided me with a feeling of worth and self-esteem unlike anything I'd ever experienced before.

That new friend's name was *basketball*.

° 2 °

Why Basketball?

Union City, New Jersey, was a hotbed of basketball when we moved there, the year I entered fifth grade. Emerson High had just gone up to Glens Falls, New York, and won the Eastern States championship, and all over town it seemed that's all people were talking about. Everywhere you looked, kids were playing basketball in schoolyards.

Basketball is, of course, a city game; some would say it's *the* city game since there's not much room for recreation in a city. (That's how fast-pitch stickball was born; it turned schoolyards into mini-baseball parks.) You'd always find the best basketball players wherever you found the best baskets, which was wherever the rims were tight, wherever the rims had nets. From time to time those locations would change. The custodian at one school would get drunk and someone would steal the nets, so you'd have to go on to the next schoolyard, though usually the custodians were smarter than that. They'd make sure there were nets in *their* yards, because that kept kids from getting into trouble. And if the kids themselves caught

11

someone stealing a net, man, they'd whack him good, really pummel him, because that meant he was screwing up their game. Nobody wanted to play without a net.

The Gilmore School was two blocks from our house, so I began hanging out there, shooting baskets by myself. Basketball's a game that has a special appeal for loners because it's a game you can work on by yourself, and I had long ago become accustomed to doing things on my own. Shooting baskets was no different to me than drawing; in a way, it was just an extension of it. There was a lot of imagination involved, and you could see yourself improving, really getting better at it, without having to be involved with anyone else. You can't do that with football or baseball; those games require groups, even for practicing. But a kid like me could amuse himself for hours and hours just tossing a ball through a hoop on an empty court.

That's what I was doing the day Perry DelPurgatorio walked into my life.

He was a highly regarded local guy who played at Villanova with Paul Arizin. In a working-class neighborhood, anyone returning home from college was looked upon as someone special, the way Tiny Archibald was years later when he returned to the South Bronx to work with street kids there. Perry had that kind of stature in Union City. Ultimately, he started some games, but when I first met him, between his junior and senior seasons, he was sort of Villanova's sixth man.

He'd come over to the Gilmore schoolyard every afternoon around five o'clock and practice by himself while the other players went home for dinner. He kept working on his outside shot, taking hundreds of them; and after watching him for a while I asked him if he wanted me to shag the ball for him.

That's how it all began.

He took a liking to me and showed me how to shoot. He explained the mechanics of it, then taught me how to make a two-hand set. Every day, all through July and August, I'd practice what he taught me, then meet him again in the afternoon to shag and learn some more.

I also got involved with a group of friends who were really into baseball. We played it all spring and summer in the PAL and the CYO, and then when fall came they formed a makeshift football team they called the Raiders. Basketball? It didn't seem to hold their interest the way that it held mine. They went from following the Yankees, Giants, and Dodgers all summer to rooting for Army and Notre Dame in the fall, and basketball was just something to fool around with when it seemed there was nothing else to do. They could take it or leave it; but I had come to enjoy it so much that shooting by myself seemed like more fun to me than going to football practice with them, which didn't endear me to them since I owned the only football.

My choice was obvious: play with them, or risk being ostracized again. But that didn't bother me anymore. I'd become a very focused person at a young age, and now that focus was squarely on basketball. Some people can point to a single moment in their lives when everything changed, when the course they were on took a fateful turn; when perhaps, as Robert Frost suggested, they opted for the road less traveled. I don't know if I can pick out such a moment in my life, but if there was one I could recognize now, it would be that first time I decided *not* to bring my football down to practice with the Raiders but to go to the schoolyard instead.

In making that decision I was telling them what I had already admitted to myself. Basketball had become my master. It was as simple as that. It had become my drug. I was as obsessed with this thing as some people are with alcohol. It was an obsession that took over my life, a true addiction, but a *good* addiction because it provided me with more than just momentary thrills; it provided me with pleasure that was both fulfilling and long-lasting.

I don't know why other guys got into the game, but I know why I got into it. The physical part of it was fun to me, and I had been taught that the way to gain acceptance and dignity was to get it first in a physical way. I was still seeking to carve out my own identity, and basketball offered me that. It presented me with a mental challenge as well as a physical challenge, but most of all it offered gratification for my ego, which at that point in my life was extremely important.

Those schoolyards became my second home. Since there were no referees there, the games tended to be like football games, to a degree. The first thing you had to do, even if you were a small kid, was to not be afraid to go after the ball, even if that meant getting hit on the head with a forehand, forearm, or elbow. I was never afraid to do that. In fact, the things I liked most about basketball as a pro were the things I liked back then. This was a game that was both physical *and* imaginative. It was a game that offered a large measure of creativity. Everything wasn't "Okay, let's go back into the huddle now. I'll call such-and-such a play, and here's what I want you to do. . . ." There was a lot more *action* in basketball than in baseball, which I found boring—standing around in right field, pounding my glove, waiting for the pitch while the sun beat down on me. In basketball you moved, you sweated. Everything seemed fluid.

The Gilmore schoolyard had a rotten backboard, a big steel rectangular thing with holes in it. After a while I got to know where every one of its dead spots was.

I also developed my hook shot there. I knew enough

to keep my body between the defender and the ball—
Perry had taught me that—and I also knew that certain defenders, once you went beyond the spot where
they thought you could bank it off the boards, would
ease up on defense, almost to the point of relaxing.
When I saw that begin to happen I went to work on
the hook, practicing it over and over until I could
make it without even using the backboard. I remember the looks I got the first few times I tried it in
games. I'd be thinking, "Yeah, baby, I know, it isn't
in the books, but relax on me and I'm gonna come up
with a shot that'll beat you!" I was like a pitcher in
baseball, sneaking in a changeup after he's fed the
batter a fastball. That's what the hook shot was for
me once I got my confidence in it. Most guys, if they
took that shot at all, would bank it off the backboard.
Sometimes I would, too. But I could also bring it
right to the baseline, where there was no backboard
to help you, where if you were going to sink a
shot you had to shoot it clean. So when defenders
started playing me to bank one, I'd wait for them
to ease up, then take it one more dribble to the baseline, and *bang!* I'd nail them with it almost every
time.

Perry returned the following summer, between my
sixth and seventh grades. He'd graduated by now,
but he still liked coming by to work out. He started
playing at fifteen dollars a game for the Woodshed
AC, a bar up the street from our house where my
father used to go for an occasional pop, and on week-
ends he'd pick up a few more dollars playing for
Bridgeport in the Eastern League. This was a guy
who really understood the game, who later became an
outstanding high school coach, and now it seemed he
was spending as much time working on my game as
he was on his own. I guess he saw potential in me,
and I think he got a kick out of teaching someone
who obviously wanted to learn.

I was growing fast. I was 5'10" by seventh grade, a big kid for my age, more agile than most of the others; I didn't fall down a lot or trip over my own feet. And now I was being taught the fundamentals of the game from a very smart college player. It was like having my own private art teacher, my own private basketball camp. He taught me essential things, like how to pass and how to dribble. I'd practice for hours in the heat of day, then he'd come by after work each night to check me out.

Basketball was taking over my life, almost to the exclusion of everything else. I spent part of *every* day working on my game, and if I had to go somewhere with my folks, like on a vacation or a long weekend somewhere, I made sure I found places to shoot. I had become what's now commonly known as a basketball junkie.

There were two courts in the Gilmore schoolyard. One was called the varsity court; the other was called the JV court. The JV court was always the court with the poorer rims, the poorer nets, or no nets at all. That was the one the younger kids used while the older guys—high school age, college age—played three-on-three. We were allowed to shag balls for them while they were warming up, but that's about as close as we ever got to the varsity court when they were around, except for running out to sneak some quick shots whenever they stopped for a drink of water. That was me, sneaking onto the varsity court with the other seventh-graders, the way you see kids sneaking onto NBA courts today when they think no one's looking.

Then came that first night when the big guys were missing a player, when someone probably didn't finish dinner soon enough, forcing them to fill a spot with one of us, and I heard them ask for me. That was no small decision. Winners got to keep the court;

losers had to leave, which meant they might not get to play again. So they weren't about to pick someone they didn't think could help them win; that would have been suicidal. I heard one of them saying, "Well, he's big, and he can shoot."

Actually, the fact I could shoot was almost immaterial, because that first time I got to play on the varsity court my instructions were these: "Set picks, okay? No shots. You can go in for rebounds, too, but remember, *no* shots." So they'd be out there scoring all the points, and I'd be putting the ball into their hands with good, crisp passes, the kind Perry taught me, which of course made them look good and didn't make me look bad at all. Occasionally, they'd pass it back and then come to me real quick, using me for a pick. When they tried to do that with some of the other young kids it wouldn't work because the kids would run rather than allow themselves to get belted. But I wouldn't budge. I'd pick them off, no matter how big they were, and after a while those older guys began to say, "Hey, this Heinsohn kid can play."

Pretty soon these juniors and seniors from high school were actually *wanting* me to play with them, which was incredibly ego-fulfilling for a seventh-grader. It was the flip side of being the neighborhood Nazi! Now, because of these basketball skills I'd acquired, the older kids began negotiating for my services and trying to be my friends, which opened up new avenues of my social life, too.

That's what Perry DelPurgatorio did for me that summer.

When winter came, those night games in the schoolyard had to move indoors, which, in Union City, meant the action now switched to the St. Joseph's Men's Club. But I was still a seventh-grader, and they wouldn't let you join until you at least got out of grammar school. Fortunately, they had a bowling alley there, so I took a job setting pins one night a week to earn some money, which my mother wanted me to do, but also to get a shot at playing on this little court they had where some of the fiercest games I've ever seen took place on a regular basis.

That's where I developed the line-drive jumper that later became my trademark with the Celtics.

This place wasn't even a gym. It was actually just a small back room with a reasonably high ceiling, perhaps eighteen feet. And it was basically square. So there was no such thing as an outside game there. It was an *inside* game exclusively—taking it to the hoop, pivot play, all of that bruising stuff. Everything was congested, yet we still played three-on-three. The football players from the high school used to love joining in because there was no such thing as finesse inside that room. The name of the game was Knock People Down! You had maybe fifteen feet in which to operate, that's all. Quickness didn't count for much. All that really mattered was how you used your body. I played in that room for several years, so I got used to being hit and to hitting back, and in the process I picked up a lot of little tricks, along with an instinct for offensive rebounds that served me well my whole career.

My father never cared much for basketball. In fact, he thought it was a sissy's game until he watched me holding my own with the big guys. Then he got excited by it and began following my development with interest and, I'm sure, a lot of pride.

By the time I was ready for high school, coaches were coming to me, trying to get me to go to their schools, which was unheard-of in those days. I had my choice of schools and my choice of coaches, so I sat down with my father and asked him what he thought I should do.

"Well, Tommy," he said, "you can go to Emerson, but you're liable to wind up as a small fish in a big pond. Or you can go to St. Michael's, where, if you're really as good as they say you are, you'll have plenty of opportunities to show it. Plus, to be honest, your mother and I would both prefer to see you go to a Catholic school.''

St. Michael's had only three hundred kids, half of whom were girls.

The next morning I called them up and told them I was coming.

○ 3 ○

The Road to Boston

Pat and Johnny Finnegan were a couple of brothers who graduated from St. Michael's and then went their separate ways in college. Pat played for Fordham, while Johnny was on those great Seton Hall teams that included Bobby Wanzer and Pep Saul. But now, with college days behind them, they'd come back home and were coaching St. Mike's *together* when I showed up.

Rumor had it the real reason they took the job was that it allowed them to use the gym for weekend workouts with their buddies from Hoboken. Whatever the reason, I was just happy they were there because the coaching was terrific and we had a lot of fun.

Like Perry DelPurgatorio, these guys knew the game. In fact, it was Johnny, who was only 5'8", who taught me a little trick for stealing balls away from big guys on a rebound that I used against Gene Wiley of the Lakers in a playoff win that gave the Celts a championship. When I give clinics now, I refer to it as "Letting the big guy show his muscles while you steal away his girlfriend." It's very simple. You just stand there, watching the guy use his force to bring the ball down, then you poke your hand at him and *pop!* the ball away. I used that trick my whole career. It was just one of many helpful techniques I learned in my years with Johnny.

Pat, meanwhile, would often get mad at me, cajoling me to push harder, to run faster, to try more, even while he was teaching me, too. He believed in me as a player so much that he rarely got off my back. There was a man who *knew* how to manage a high school kid.

By my senior season I had grown to 6'4" and my arsenal now included a hook shot, an inside shot, an outside shot, offensive rebounds, layups, instinctive moves in the pivot; it was all coming together fast. We went to Brooklyn and won the Metropolitan Catholic championship, then we went to Newport for the ESCIT (Eastern States Catholic Invitational Tournament). This was heady stuff for a tiny school like St. Michael's, getting invited to the ESCIT along with parochial powerhouses from Chicago, New York, Washington, and Trenton. We lost to All Hallows but we didn't embarrass ourselves at all. Then we came home to win the Hudson County championship, a major prize, before losing the state championship to St. Peter's with its one thousand boys, in the final game of the New Jersey schoolboy tournament.

Not bad for a coed school of three hundred.

We played so much that by the end of my senior season I had lost 25 pounds and looked like Kevin McHale, on top of which I had the flu and felt like a dog. But I also had scholarship offers from more than a hundred colleges.

Recruiting back then was nothing like it is today, where they send out assistant coaches to woo you and the *head* coach if you're really special. It was more sectional than regional in those days. Yet I could have gone to almost any school I wanted to in the country.

I went to Holy Cross, a Jesuit college in Worcester, Massachusetts, forty miles from Boston, primarily because I thought I wanted to be a doctor. Everybody else was promising me the sun, the moon, and the stars—''Yeah, we'll take your girlfriend! Sure, we'll put you through medical school. . . .''—while the admissions people I met at the Cross were right up front in telling me it was extremely difficult for an athlete to compete in a varsity sport and still maintain the grades he'd need to complete their premed course. They said they really didn't believe I could do it, so if I was going to be adamant about it they'd probably have to rescind their offer.

That's the biggest reason I went there: I appreciated that they leveled with me, and I recognized that they were probably right. And I guess I was also influenced by the fact they already had two Hudson County guys on the team, Togo Palazzi, whom I later played with on the Celtics, and Earl Markey, now a Jesuit there, who was captain and an honorable-mention All-American.

In my sophomore year we went 26–2, beating Bob Pettit's LSU team for the Sugar Bowl championship, then beating Duquesne, ranked second in the nation, 71–62, for the NIT championship, which in those days was *the* championship to win, much more prestigious than the NCAA. I had 20 points in the win over Duquesne. So did Togo. Then he graduted, along with Ronnie Perry, another key player, which meant it was rebuilding time at the Cross.

My junior season wasn't bad either at 19–7; it just wasn't as good as what I'd experienced the year before, though I won the MVP in our Sugar Bowl loss to Notre Dame. We also wound up losing to Maurice Stokes's St. Francis club in the NCAA. Even worse for me, we lost our coach, Buster Sheary, when he had a falling-out with officials in the school administration.

They brought in a prep-school coach from New Jersey, Roy Leenig, giving him his first crack at coaching on a major college level in what was supposed to be a great season for us. Statistically it was—22–5 —but he and I just never hit it off. The truth was, I didn't think he knew what he was doing, especially when he'd prepare us for games with scouting reports he'd written on the backs of matchbook covers. There was no way in the world he was ready to coach that team. Still, we managed to coexist all right until the day he tried to make me the scapegoat for our failure to do what no one else in college basketball had been able to do for two years, namely, beat Bill Russell.

We had our shot at him, and we got our heads handed to us, 67–51.

Leenig just wouldn't accept the fact we couldn't beat him. But I had no trouble accepting it. Then again, I had better reason to accept it. I was the guy who had to play him.

It was the Holiday Festival at Madison Square Garden and the showdown attracted an inordinate amount of attention, even by New York standards, because by this time I was generally acknowledged as the best player on the East Coast, one of the best in the East overall, and here we were going up against this team from San Francisco that no one heard very much about, except for the fact it had a mysterious big black guy in the middle and was still unbeaten in its drive to win back-to-back NCAA championships.

The duel was going to be between Russell and me. I knew it, and he knew it, too. And knowing what I know about him now, knowing how he reacts whenever that pride of his gets wounded, I can just imagine what was going through his mind as we got ready to square off that night: *Hey, I'm ten times better than this white guy everyone's writing about!* That would have been more than enough to get his juices cooking. But it was also coupled with the fact that people in this part of the country—basketball people who should have known better, who should have realized that records like his couldn't have been fashioned out of chopped liver—tended to regard San Francisco's accomplishments as some sort of fluke, some sort of aberration that would be quickly reconciled the moment the Dons hooked up with a *legitimate* power from the East, like that Jesuit school in Worcester.

As if all that wasn't bad enough, Leenig started yapping to the press, PRing the confrontation! Russell must have been dying to get his hands on me.

We were still using Buster Sheary's 3–2 spread offense, an offense designed to pull out the defense, in which the center, me, became another ballhandler. That's how we started the game, which meant we now had Russell pulled out of the middle so he couldn't block any shots. It was working fine; I was hitting guys for easy layups, plus I scored 10 points myself in the opening quarter. Meanwhile, however, I had to guard Russell when we all got down to his end, and he and KC Jones had cooked up this little play that was perfectly legal back then. KC would dribble into a corner and make believe he was gettig ready to take a shot, then throw the ball right over the top of the backboard, where Russell would catch it and cram it home. He had that kind of leaping ability, so there was no way to defend that shot; it was like a free two points each time they tried it.

No one I ever played against had done anything like that before. But now I caught on to what they were doing, and I realized the only way to stop it was to muscle Russell out of position, so I started banging on him, really getting physical, and he started banging back. He wasn't too happy about it, but Russell never backed down from anyone.

The first half ended and we were up by three,

32–29. I was running the offense, pulling out the defense, bounce-passing to guys on reverse cuts, sending them in for layups, and I'd gotten a dozen points of my own. I was having a hell of a time, but in the process of jockeying with Russell I also picked up three fouls, so when the second half started we had to bring in a sophomore center named Pete Houston to do the banging.

As soon as they realized he was no factor at all on offense they began backing off, picking up our cutters, using Houston's man to jam the middle. Our attack was suddenly stagnant, so there was only one thing left for me to do, and that was to go one-on-one with Russell.

I gave him one of my best fakes. Faking was a big part of my game. When I faked guys, that was it; good-bye, see you later! I'd be gone. So now I faked Russell—left him standing five feet away—and I headed for the basket when, *whack,* he batted the ball right out of my hands! I was thinking, *Where the hell did he come from?* Then he did it again, and again, and now I was shooting hook shots and the sonofabitch was blocking those! I had never met anyone like him before in my life. He did a total number on me; just took my game away. I didn't score a single point in the whole second half, while he wound up with 24 for the night.

The next time I saw him the two of us were on the same team. Thank God.

The following morning, as we practiced in the Sixty-ninth Regiment Armory for our consolation game with Duquesne, Leenig made a big production out of assigning me to the second team, right in front of the writers, as if somehow I had been personally responsible for the loss to San Francisco. I guess he thought I had gone off on my own, which I had to a degree; but, hell, nobody else seemed anxious to make something happen and we were getting our butts kicked.

He started berating me, saying, "This is *not* a one-man show!" I told him I understood that, but he stayed on my case so much that he had me almost ready to quit. I went home and talked to my folks about the possibility of finishing school somewhere else. But my father was cool. He just listened, allowing me to vent my anger, because he knew I was going to go back.

I did, but now a lot of the enjoyment was gone and I was simply marking time to see what might lie around the corner after graduation.

I made all of the All-American teams that spring and went on tour with the Globetrotters. When I returned I learned that the Celtics planned to make me their territorial pick in the draft, which everyone, including me, had more or less expected. In those days NBA teams were granted proprietary rights to players who attended nearby colleges, the assumption being these local favorites might bring with them the loyalty and support of fans who hadn't yet developed an appetite for the game at a professional level.

Boston was basically a two-team town in 1956. The Red Sox and Bruins had both been around since the inception of their leagues, so the roots of baseball and hockey ran deep. The Celtics had been around since the beginning of their league, too, but that league was only ten years old when Red Auerbach told the writers he was going to pick me—*if I got rid of the fat!*

I didn't like that. I was 6'7" and weighed 235 pounds, and frankly, I thought I was in great shape. Then I picked up the papers and read where he said I was out of shape, and that unless I got down to 218 I'd probably be of no use to him. "This guy's got no business weighing 235," he told one paper. "But when you're a big star in college you get to thinking you're indispensable, that you can do any damned thing you want. Well, that doesn't go up here!"

I took it to heart and caught a flight to Illinois the

next day to meet with officials of the AAU's Peoria Caterpillars, who had offered me a chance to play with them. When I got home there was a message waiting, tellng me to call Bob Cousy.

Cooz had played at Holy Cross, too, but by the time I arrived he was already a major star in the NBA. I watched him on television a lot, and once went down to Worcester Auditorium as a sophomore to see him in an exhibition game; but I didn't actually meet him until my junior year.

"Tommy," he said when I called him back, "don't pay any attention to that stuff. That's just Red's way. It's newspaper talk, that's all. Believe me, he *wants* you. I'll pick you up in the morning and take you in to meet him."

I was only a part of Auerbach's plans for the following season. In addition to taking me as a territorial pick, he swung a gutsy deal in which he sent Ed Macauley, his high-scoring center and perennial all-star, to the St. Louis Hawks along with the rights to Cliff Hagan, the great forward from Kentucky who was just getting out of the service. Red had drafted Hagan a couple of years earlier, even knowing he wouldn't be able to use him until his military duties were over. Now Cliff was coming home.

It was a tremendous package he was offering the Hawks, and all he wanted in return was their first pick in the draft, which would be the number two pick overall. Rochester, picking first, had already gone on record as saying it would take Sihugo Green, the guard from Duquesne.

That was fine with Auerbach. He had someone else in mind. He planned to use the pick, he said, to acquire another center, someone from San Francisco named Russell.

Cousy was right. My meeting with Auerbach went well, very well. We agreed on a contract right away, and then he called a big press conference to announce

I was now a Celtic. I spent more than half of that conference answering questions about Russell, telling everybody how great I thought he was and assuring the ones who didn't know much about him that they were in for a very pleasant surprise.

We all were.

The Yankees won the World Series five times in a row. They did that twice. And the Canadiens won the Stanley Cup five times in a row. They also did that twice. But we were about to launch a dynasty like no other dynasty professional sports had ever seen, or has seen since. It would last thirteen years and claim eleven championships, eight of which we won in succession.

There was, of course, no way of anticipating anything like that the day I signed with the Celtics.

I simply had a feeling something good was going to happen.

° 4 °

Save the Women and Children!

I can teach someone to enjoy and understand basketball in five minutes. That's really all it takes, because
it's not a complicated game.

Oh, some people like to make it complicated. Listen to Hubie Brown whenever he's a guest analyst on
network telecasts. He hits his viewers with so much
technical crap that by the third quarter even a very
knowledgeable fan can't bear to listen anymore.

Hubie, please, enough already!

See, he forgets all about the entertainment value of
the game, and it *is* an entertaining game.

It's two plus two equals four, all right? It's *not* E
equals MC squared, although there are elements of
that in it. There are also elements of geometry and
bits of algebra, too; but as long as you understand the
basics of it, that two plus two equals four, you can
follow any game with interest and enjoyment.

Remember, we're not discussing the theory of rela-
tivity here. We're talking basketball, that's all. And
since we're about to move into the nitty-gritty of this
book—memories, lessons, and reflections gathered over

thirty years of playing, coaching, and broadcasting—this might be an appropriate spot to pause for a crash course on strategies and terminology, just to make the following pages more meaningful for anyone coming in late.

If that's *you*, welcome aboard!

Basketball is a game that has two principal elements: size and speed.

The first element you try to capitalize on is speed. There are five guys on each team, and the idea is to see how quickly your side, once it gains possession of the ball, can get its members up the court, penetrating the other team's defense in order to create numerical advantages in which you have a one- or two-man edge over the players who stand between you and the basket. You create those advantages by using speed. It's called a *fast break*, and certain teams—the current Lakers are a great example—train hard to create and exploit those situations all the time.

If you can't create a numerical advantage through speed, the next thing you look for is size. But size is generally important only within 10 feet of the basket, 15 feet sometimes. Size allows a man to be closer to the basket and therefore to have perhaps a higher percentage of shooting accuracy. The closer you are to the basket, the easier it should be to score. So people sometimes mistakenly assume that size is *all* there is to basketball. But there are various defenses designed to take away that size advantage, to nullify what's commonly known as the *inside game*. When that happens, when a defense shuts down your inside game, you have to go to what's called the *outside game*, which consists of shooting from a distance.

The good teams have both an *inside* and an *outside* game. If they place a big guy under the basket, the defense automatically contracts around him, which means that some of his teammates are going to be left alone outside. Now if they can take the ball and score from out there before the defense comes out to guard them, hey, it's worth the same two points they would have gotten if the big guy dropped the ball into the bucket instead. And this is what is going on throughout the course of most games. You're constantly trying to pull the defense inside or outside, forcing it to react to whatever you're doing.

That's basketball—the two plus two equals four aspect of it.

One of the fundamental skills required in the game is rebounding. Rebounding is important because, if you're a good *offensive* rebounder, it will enable your team to occasionally get an extra shot at a basket, a shot it otherwise wouldn't have had. And if you're a good *defensive* rebounder, you're able to deny your opposition that extra shot. The advantage in these battles normally goes to the defensive rebounder because he's able to establish a position between the offensive rebounder and the basket. After that, all that's generally required of him is a little bit of blocking out.

The essence of a great rebounder, in my opinion, is the offensive rebounder, the guy who has to fight for that good position, who has to come up with all kinds of little tricks in order to regain the advantage. The really great offensive rebounder has an aggressiveness in his makeup that causes him to say to himself, "I am not giving up my pursuit of this ball until that other team absolutely has possession of it."

He's like a Mack truck turned loose. He'll bull you, he'll push you, he'll ride you in; you can't allow him any room because, if you do, he'll just bowl you over. When I give lectures to kids I tell them: "Stop the Mack truck and save the women and children!" That's what an offensive rebounder is like; he's like a Mack truck whose brakes have let loose and now it's going to run over the women and children, anything that gets in its way. So how do you save the women and children? Simple. You've got to slow down that truck and put on its brakes before it gets rolling too fast.

First you try to *block it out*. That's a basketball term for getting in its way. If you can't do that, then you try to divert it; if you can force it down the driveway and into the garage where you can then contain it, hey, you've saved the women and children!

That's what the defensive rebounder tries to do. He gets his arm up—his arm is the driveway—and as this truck starts running up his arm, he spins it onto his back; his back's the garage. And then with his other arm, his away arm, he locks the door. That's defensive rebounding.

But Mack trucks are smart. They've got all kinds of moves. Their wheels may spin a little bit, their fenders may come into your sides as you're pushing them toward the garage, hoping they can bounce off the guardrail into the direction of the basket. You constantly have to keep your driveway moving, keep your feet going, until you know the Mack truck's been contained. You never lock the door until you're sure it's in the garage.

Then there are the *Walls of Troy*.

We're talking about the mechanics of shooting now. There are certain precepts that apply. If you were going to shoot a rifle, you'd put your eye right over the barrel of the gun, then line it up with the sight and the target. It's the same idea when you shoot a basketball. You line up your eye with the sight, which is the basket. The theory of shooting is that everything falls into a straight line.

The second aspect of it is that there are certain springs involved. Your fingers, your wrists, your elbows, your knees are all springs, and if you can bring them all into play when you shoot, distance will not be as much of a factor because each spring provides additional power. The biggest springs, your knees, are what give you the distance on your shots; that's where most of your spring action should be. If you have exaggerated spring action in your fingers or wrists, the ball will be released too hard.

The spring action in your legs is like a catapult in the Trojan War. The city's besieged, and now we're going to throw these flaming rocks over the walls to finish the job, to destroy it. But in order to catapult these fiery targets over the wall, everything has to be in a straight line. If your elbow's flying out, if your hand isn't under the ball, if your body isn't behind it, you're going to fall short. That's what shooting's all about. Imagine a fiery rock leaving a catapult and going *Pffft!* Or going way off target because the springs are crooked.

We want those fiery balls soaring over the walls and making direct hits on their targets, because that's our *outside game* and we're going to need to have it working if we're going to win this war.

If we can just make the defenders come out from behind those walls to stop us from firing these missiles, the battle will be half-won.

Nothing demoralizes the opposition any quicker than an effective fast break. After the defenders have been outnumbered two or three times in rapid succession they begin to feel a bit like General Custer's men at the Battle of Little Bighorn: *Where the hell did all of these Indians come from?* It's the most helpless feeling in the world to see three-on-twos and four-on-threes coming at you all night long: "We're expected to stop all these guys?" It's impossible, so you call a timeout and go back to your huddle and start arguing with your teammates: "Why aren't you there, where you were supposed to be, Major Reno?" Only Custer never got a chance to ask Major Reno where he was with the anticipated help, because Major Reno never showed up.

We saw that same helpless look in the eyes of many opponents many times with the great fast break we had in Boston.

If it's an *inside game* you're called upon to stop,

what you want to do is cut down some of those trees. That's what I call those guys who play the inside game: the Tall Timber.

So how do you stop these trees from doing damage to you? Simple. You don't let them have the ball, and there are various ways to deny it to them. You can deny them the angle of the pass, which forces the big guy to shoot from farther out than he likes to be. You make it a more difficult shot that way. Or you block him off the offensive boards so that he can't get an extra shot by using his size. And if he does get the ball, you can try forcing him to his weakness, which means analyzing him. If he likes to do *this,* make him do *that!* For instance, if he's a right-handed shooter, try forcing him to use his left hand, his poorer hand, instead.

Those are just some of the ways to go about chopping down trees. "Tim-ber!"

Fast break. Outside. Inside. Size. Speed.
Do you see what I mean? It's not a complicated game at all as long as you understand its basic elements. It then becomes a simple matter of who can execute them best; or, if you're looking through the eyes of a hoop connoisseur, who you most enjoy watching.

In either case, you're going to find yourself faced with a remarkable selection, because this is a game that's played by the finest athletes in the world.

And why not? It's the greatest game in town.

○ 5 ○

Evolution

Pro basketball was changing rapidly when I arrived. Still, it wasn't all that far removed from the dance-hall era when guys would play for nickels and dimes as soon as Benny Goodman called it quits for the night. As a professional sport, its appeal in the 1920s and 1930s was largely limited to touring teams, like the Original Celtics from New York with Joe Lapchick, Nat Holman, and Dutch Dehnert; the New York Whirlwinds; the all-black Rens (Renaissance), also from New York; and the Philadelphia Spahs (South Philadelphia Hebrew Association).

But when World War II came along, it brought together groups of guys from all over the country who found an immediate common interest in this sport that was so easy to play. Balls and hoops took up almost no space, and games could be organized on a moment's notice. So it became the soldiers' game for some of the same reasons it became the city game. When the war finally ended there was a great mass of ex-servicemen heading off to colleges, intent on continuing a love affair with basketball.

We had become a pretty wealthy country by that time, and now colleges that once stressed football were beginning to turn their attention to this other game. When I got out of high school in 1952, just seven years after the armistice, recruiting was nowhere near as sophisticated as it is today, but it was clearly moving in that direction.

Madison Square Garden was basketball's Mecca. It not only hosted the NIT, which was the major event of the year back then, but it also promoted college doubleheaders that regularly sold out, making them the figurehead of this new rage sweeping across the country. Colleges, of course, have the immeasurable advantage of a built-in audience, a loyal army of fans at each university who would gladly support a tiddly-winks tournament if *their* team were involved.

It was a market any entrepreneur would love to tap, and so it was that today's National Basketball Association was born of the belief, or at least the hope, that former college stars might bring with them enduring links to alumni dollars, that loyalties forged in undergrad days might follow them into their careers as pros. It was a theory that didn't hold water but was nevertheless sufficient to bring about a 1949 marriage between the National Basketball League, which was teetering, and the Basketball Association of America, which had been raiding the older league's teams and players since its own inception three years earlier.

Among the earliest members of the BAA were the New York Knickerbockers and the Boston Celtics, the only charter teams still in their original locations today. Most of its founders were hockey people who, seeing the bullish market that existed for college basketball, thought it only prudent, if not downright ingenious, to establish a professional facsimile and so eliminate dark nights in their buildings. With a few notable exceptions—Red Auerbach, who, fresh out of the navy, talked his way into the coaching job at Washington at the age of twenty-nine; Ned Irish, who promoted those doubleheaders at Madison Square Garden; and Eddie Gottlieb, who coached the Spahs in Philadelphia, then later owned the Warriors—these were all hockey people who admittedly knew precious little about the sport. When it came time for them to pick their first commissioner, they gave the post to Maurice Podoloff, whose chief credential was that he had done a decent job as president of the American Hockey League.

On the basis of that information alone we can reasonably conclude that if baseball has to be a marvelous game in order to have survived the people who've run it, basketball must be the greatest game in history.

It took a long time for the pro game to click, however.

First, in order to develop mass appeal it had to get established in major cities; Fort Wayne, Sheboygan, and Oshkosh simply weren't going to make it, nor were Rochester, Providence, or the immortal Tri-Cities. It took time, but gradually those needed changes were made—St. Louis came into the league in 1955, replacing Milwaukee; the Pistons left Fort Wayne for Detroit in 1957—and little by little momentum built up, first along the East Coast, then throughout the Midwest. Still, even a great team like those Minneapolis Lakers who won five championships with George Mikan wasn't well-known to vast numbers of people. "The Lakers? Mikkelsen, Pollard, and Mikan? Who are they? Where do they play?" people would ask. Nobody watched TV the way people do today because TV, like the league, was still in its infancy.

The Knicks were the first team to really catch on big, primarily because the sport already enjoyed a good base in New York, but also because Ned Irish was perceptive enough to stock his club with well-known stars from local schools, like Carl Braun and Ernie Vandeweghe from Colgate and Dick McGuire from St. John's, though he had some pretty good interlopers, too, like Harry "the Horse" Gallatin from Northeast Missouri. I can remember getting very excited about that team around 1950.

But the guy who really made the sport was the guy they called *Mister Basketball*, Bob Cousy. He was the flashiest player in the entire league—a great, great playmaker; the master of the behind-the-back-pass—and by the time I got to Holy Cross, kids who put on fancy moves were already being chided with: "Hey, who do you think you are, The Cooz?"

If there was a single development that changed the course of NBA history, it had to have been the introduction of the twenty-four-second shot clock in the 1954–55 season. Ironically, in later years that same clock would come to be the source of a widespread criticism you still hear today, namely that all you have to do is watch the last two minutes of any pro game to get a handle on what's happening. That's nonsense.

What the shot clock did was guarantee there would be forty-eight minutes of action, which fans certainly weren't getting in those preclock days when the way to thwart a fast break was to hold the ball all night. Now you had to relinquish possession, so what resulted was a forced tempo, an acceleration of the pace of every game.

Fast-break basketball had been around a long time Frank Keaney's teams at the University of Rhode Island were playing "racehorse" basketball as far back as the 1930s, though they enjoyed their greatest prominence during the Ernie Calverley era of the mid-1940s. Eddie Hickey's teams at St. Louis University were playing fast-break ball back then, too. So were teams at Indiana. And high school teams all over New Jersey were certainly playing it while I was there; I know, because my team was one of them.

Now the pros were wising up, making a formal commitment, if not to fast-break ball, then at least to a game that guaranteed crowd-pleasing action, that guaranteed no one could run away with the ball and hide all night.

Styles changed because of it, new strategies were developed, and the teams that prospered most were the ones that knew how to move the ball and wear down the opposition, that knew how to break open a game with bursts of speed and with clusters of points.

The accent was now on mobility, on stamina, on creativity, and for one team in particular it would prove to be a format made to order, an imposed style that fit like a custom-tailored suit.

That team was the Celtics team I joined in the fall of 1956.

Our championship reign began in 1956–57. Elgin Baylor showed up in 1958–59, followed by Wilt Chamberlain in 1959–60. Then Oscar Robertson and Jerry West came onto the scene in 1960–61, the same year the Lakers left Minneapolis for Los Angeles. Now the NBA not only had a growing number of household names, but basketball was also truly a national sport in every sense. Baseball was still America's favorite pastime; and football, on the strength of a historic championship game between the Colts and Giants in 1958, was coming on strong, but at least the stage had been set for professional basketball to finally come out of the shadows.

The 1960s were fabulous years to play in the NBA, for reasons, I might add, that had little to do with money.

Did you ever wonder what happened to all those prospectors who went to California in search of gold and found no gold? That was us. Oh, a few got rich, not many, but we *all* enjoyed the California sunshine.

I have a real fondness in my heart for the players from that era. By today's standards there was no money back then, so guys played for the best reason of all: They genuinely loved the game. That was the common bond. They weren't in it for the money because there was no money. They were in it for the life-style and because it was something they did well, something that they understood. They were all competitive people who loved the game for what it said about them and for what it represented to them.

When people talk about the "motivation" of the modern athlete, the question I always have to ask is: *Why are they in the game?* Some of them, I think, are in it only for the dough. Sure, within the framework of the current NBA I can spot a lot of players who'd still be out there if they weren't making serious dollars—but I can also spot a few who'd never be there if they weren't pulling down a million dollars.

We used to look at guys like Ted Williams and Joe DiMaggio, who were reportedly making as much as $100,000 a season, and we'd say to ourselves, "Boy, isn't that incredible?" I played for $9,000 in my rookie season, and that was considered a lot of money. We always believed the day would come when basketball would offer fortunes, too, because we believed in the game, but we also understood it probably wasn't going to happen in our time. Our job was to sell the product; someone else would reap the profits. KC Jones retired in 1967 when he could have played more. Why? Because he couldn't afford to stay. He could make more money on the outside than he could playing ball. And he certainly wasn't the only one in that boat. I made more money on the outside, in the insurance business, while I was playing for the Celtics than I ever made in salary, and I was one of the top-paid guys on the team.

That's what I mean when I say the players in those days had a real love for the game.

They also enjoyed the camaraderie, which was a lot different then than it is today. Doubleheaders, the kind they had in college, were common when I came into the league. We played them all the time, which meant you'd often pull into a town and find three other teams already there. You'd walk into the hotel lounge or the all-night diner and it would seem like half of the NBA was sitting there. So it wasn't unusual for players from different teams to end up spending a great deal of time together. I had wonderful road friendships, lots of fun, a million laughs with people like Carl Braun, Johnny Kerr, Al Bianchi, Richie Guerin—*until* the games started, and then the fur flew.

Perhaps it's a sign of age to say I wish kids understood today what those guys did for the game back then. I don't know, maybe you had to have been personally involved. Hell, try telling kids about Hitler today, about what an impact *that* man had on the world, and the reasons why it happened, and they can't comprehend it, even though it's written down in books. It's of no relevance to them because they didn't participate in it; the only way they're ever going to participate is in a storybook fashion, which leaves them asking, *Fine, but what does that have to do with me?* And if they can't comprehend something as awful as that, then maybe I shouldn't expect them to comprehend the things I'm talking about here, the nice things, the homespun things, the beautiful things that era represented.

But I do wish they'd at least appreciate them.

By the end of the 1960s it was evident the NBA was about to blossom, yet in the 1970s it never happened.

The league was approached by people wanting to buy in, and when they got rebuffed they decided to set up a league of their own which they called the American Basketball Association. It was born in February 1967, and it died through absorption into the NBA in June 1976, but during the nine years of its existence it changed the face of pro basketball forever. Bidding wars broke out, the results of which were outrageous contracts being offered to established NBA stars in an effort to lure them away, to give the new league credibility and identity.

Meanwhile, the NBA was getting greedy, too. The old owners were dying off. Men like Ned Irish, Eddie Gottlieb, and Walter Brown in Boston were disappearing from the scene, and their places were being taken by a new breed of owner who had no idea what the game had been like in those years we were winning all those championships. These new moguls took one look at all those buyers lining up with money in their hands and said, "Hey, this is great! Let's charge them as much as we can and bring them in." Now, in addition to salary wars and player raids, the NBA was further weakened by the self-inflicted wounds of expansion.

When I played it seemed every team was nine-deep in talent, some ten-deep. Whenever I stepped out of the lineup, a Willie Naulls stepped in. You were replaced by someone almost as good as you were. Six of our regulars—Bob Cousy, Bill Russell, Bill Sharman, Frank Ramsey, Sam Jones, and me; and later a seventh, John Havlicek—wound up in the Hall of Fame. I joined a league of eighty players. Granted, skills have improved with each succeeding generation, but that's been offset by a watering-down of rosters. Today you rarely see a team with five top players; some are lucky to have even three. And now this season, with Miami and Charlotte increasing the number of franchises to twenty-five, the number of players in the NBA will jump from 276 to 300, with Minneapolis and Orlando waiting on deck to join the party next year.

During the nine years I played I attended practically every league meeting as a representative of the Players Association. When they first started having those meetings we could have held them in a coffee shop. The last one I attended, in 1978, which I went to as a representative of the Coaches Association, was held in San Diego and looked like a meeting of the United Nations! They had filled a huge room with a U-shaped table and every owner had his support personnel lined up behind him in a triangle. There were lawyers! Accountants! It was incredible. I can remember looking around at all those blank faces and smiling to myself as I thought, *What would the league's old-timers have said about this?*

The man who emerged as giant in all that confusion, in my eyes anyway, was Larry O'Brien, the NBA's third commissioner. Podoloff, who was not a very pleasant man to be around, certainly helped the league's early growth under trying circumstances, and it was under his administration that it secured its first TV contract in 1954. Podoloff retired in 1963, after seventeen years on the job, and was replaced by a more imaginative man, a man with a lot more flair, Walter Kennedy. Under his leadership the league got its first *national* TV contract, but, not being as dictatorial as Podoloff, Kennedy eventually succumbed to new-breed owners looking to feather their own nests through the windfalls of expansion.

O'Brien, a confidant of the late President John F. Kennedy, took over in 1975–76. The league by then had ballooned to eighteen teams, yet its war with the ABA still raged and everyone was getting hurt in the crossfire. A skilled politician who had a gift for hard negotiations, along with the broad vision needed in those times, O'Brien knew how to deal with all these individual egos, how to get them all focused on the same goal. He brought the warring factions together and consummated a merger during his first year in office. He also demonstrated strength in his dealings with the players, who by then had created a strong bargaining unit. He showed them he respected them, yet he made it clear he wasn't afraid of them.

But most of all, he stole a page from the NFL's book and began to merchandise the product, to market the NBA in a way that had never been attempted before. Under his inspired direction, the game that started out in dance halls finally went over the top.

If Benny Goodman were alive today, they might let him play at halftime.

° 6 °

Boot Camp

I showed up for my first Celtics camp weighing 216, down from the 235 I weighed when I left Holy Cross, and Auerbach seemed pleased, though I still didn't see where it was all that big a deal.

But I was about to find out.

The first two days of camp caused me no problems. I went through all the drills and thought I handled them pretty well. They were designed to get you running faster, faster, all the time faster. Every session was predicated on that. You'd start off at a trot, then crank it up to what you thought was full speed, at which point Auerbach would start yelling for you to *accelerate!* Now you were running as fast as you possibly could, which was not only what he wanted, it was what he demanded.

The phone in my room at the Lenox Hotel rang with a wakeup call the morning of my third day at camp. I shook the cobwebs out of my head, then rolled out of bed, the way I always did, and the minute my feet hit the floor . . . *there wasn't one muscle in my body that didn't ache!* I mean, I shivered with pain! I tried to straighten up and it was like "Wow, something's wrong, this shouldn't be happening to me." I'd worked out every day that summer, getting the weight down the way Auerbach told me to, and I thought I was in fantastic shape. But now I could barely bend my legs to put my pants on, so I got dressed as best I could, then made my way to camp, where I crawled up onto the trainer's table and waited for Red, figuring he'd be as worried as I was when he arrived and saw me suffering.

Then everyone else began showing up, and pretty soon it was obvious I wasn't the only hurtin' dude there. They all looked as sore as I did. Some looked worse. As the years went by we'd laugh about this, watching new kids—or, even better, some of the veterans we picked up—go through those first few days of camp with smiles on their faces, then suddenly walk in one morning looking like the Frankenstein monster.

That happened to Willie Naulls when he joined us in 1963, only in his case it didn't take three days. It didn't even take three hours! He'd been in the league seven years by that time and thought he knew the ropes, thought he'd seen just about everything. But he'd never seen an Auerbach training camp, much less experienced one for himself. He did all right that first morning, but later that afternoon Red had us running and jumping all over the Babson College gym. Then, with no rest, he ordered us onto the floor and demanded situps. Well, that was too much for Willie. First the poor guy puked, then he passed out. Red ordered us to drag him over to a corner, where we left him, and then the workout continued.

Auerbach's plan was to torture anyone not in superlative shape, and he made no bones about it. He had it very well planned in his mind, very well timed. He'd diversify the drills so you were never quite sure what was coming, and then he'd watch you like a hawk, trying to see how different guys reacted. My reaction, or at least my inclination, that third morning of my first time at camp was to run a white flag up the pole, to hide, to do anything I could to get away from this guy, because I knew that whatever he was going to ask me to do would hurt, and if I was hurting *this* bad now, what was I going to feel like when the next workout ended? I probably wouldn't be able to crawl out of the gym on my hands and knees!

But you didn't challenge Red. You didn't question him. The only thing I ever bucked him on was push-ups. I still can't do push-ups. I never could. I don't know, maybe I've got the wrong center of gravity or something. What's more, I thoroughly believed they'd ruin my shooting touch. It was a belief I developed in high school and college when I'd spend my summers working out on the docks, unloading freight cars. I'd build up the top part of my body that way, but every time I did that it seemed I'd lose my touch. That's what I told Red. But he didn't believe me. He made me do them anyway. So whenever he wasn't looking, I'd cheat. I wouldn't do them. And I wasn't the only one cheating. Cousy cheated, too. The only guy who really did them right was Bill Sharman, which figured.

Sharman was the epitome of the perfectly conditioned athlete, right down to carrying vitamin pills in his suitcase. He was the most organized athlete I ever saw in terms of his physical regimen, way ahead of his time. He'd go to the gym for a light shoot-around on the morning of a game, all by himself. No one else did that back then. When he took over as coach of the Lakers in 1971 he had his whole team do it. Now *all* teams do it.

How precise was this man? We pulled into Minneapolis late one afternoon because of a snowstorm, leaving us three hours to rest before heading to the game. We were scheduled to fly out right afterward, so Cooz, Sharman, and I were assigned a room to grab whatever rest we could. Sharman proceeds to open his suitcase, put all of his clothes neatly into a drawer—shirts, underwear, socks, everything—and then three hours later he takes them out and packs the suitcase again. That's how precise he was.

Cousy got hurt once and I ended up rooming with Sharman on a four-game trip. He had everything down to a routine. He'd eat at the same time every day, nap at the same time, and get a certain number of hours' sleep every night. Not wanting to disturb him by coming and going every couple of hours, I tried adjusting to his pattern. I never slept so much in my entire life! When I got off the plane at the end of the trip and fell asleep in the car my wife looked at me and said, "Boy, you must have had a good ol' time on the road." I said, "You won't believe this, but all I did was sleep." That's why I couldn't stay awake: After four days with Sharman my body was starving for oxygen.

So push-ups were no problem for Bill. He'd be doing them perfectly, even while Red's back was turned, when the rest of us were trying to steal a breather. Whenever Red caught me doing that he'd stand right over me, ordering me to try harder, and everyone else would laugh because they knew I was trying as hard as I could.

We did none of those stretching exercises you see guys doing today, no aerobics or anything like that. Who ever heard of aerobics back then? We jogged a little, then we did calisthenics—jumping jacks and all that crap. Most of all, we ran. Boy, did we run! But Red was careful, too. After a few days he'd make sure he gave us extra time to loosen up, then he'd watch us closely because he didn't want anyone popping hamstrings, though we always popped a few.

I was never what you'd call a speed merchant. I hated running almost as much as I hated push-ups. But Red had been sort of a drill instructor in the navy—an officer in charge of physical fitness—and he brought a lot of that training into his coaching career. He believed he could get a jump on the rest of the league if his team was in superior condition when it left camp. Other teams would play their way into shape once the season got started. Not the Celtics. Red's team would *be* in shape right from the very get-go. He was totally committed to that approach.

But getting a jump on the opposition was really just a plus, just a byproduct of his training camp regimen. What he really wanted to do was get us psychologically prepared to play his style of basketball for forty-eight minutes a game. An Auerbach team never rested. That was like an article of faith to him. While the stated philosophy of other coaches was to "slow it down," to conserve strength, to be careful not to expend all your energy too early in the game, Red's idea was to keep everyone putting out 100 percent, all the time, with replacements coming off the bench as needed to maintain that exhausting pace.

That's why "roles" became so important on the Celtics, why Red was so careful to PR them in the papers every chance he got. If you were going to play this kind of basketball all season long, which we did, you obviously were going to need input from every member of the team. Yet everyone couldn't have a leading role. That was impossible. There had to be character actors, too, so in order to make sure that everyone felt fulfilled with the part he had in the script, Red would go out of his way to point out seemingly minor contributions to the writers. This didn't go unnoticed in the locker room.

People are always giving Red credit for being a basketball genius, which he is. But more than that, he was a management genius, too. Hundreds of his ideas actually came from his players, but he was smart enough to solicit those ideas, to welcome and consider them and then to fit them into his overall scheme of things, to make them work.

That was one of the first things I noticed about playing for Red, once I got beyond the pain. It was obvious he was interested in what I thought, in what we all thought. Consequently, we began to feel free to make suggestions, to offer opinions, not in matters of discipline or authority—it was always understood who the boss was—but in matters relating to what was happening out there on the court.

That's something you don't see very often at any level of sports, but it was a common practice on our team. There'd be a timeout and Red would say, "Okay, Cooz, what do you think?" Or, "Let's try Tommy's play now." We were all allowed to have creative input. We weren't just robots, just hired hands waiting to be told what to do. We were urged to get involved in the thought process, to look for things that might work and then bring them to the team's attention. Some suggestions were readily embraced, while others were rejected, but you never had to fear that something you recommended would be rejected out of hand. You always knew whatever you had to say would be carefully weighed, that all suggestions would be duly considered before the final decision was made by Red.

This was not only important to the so-called "role" players, it was just as important to the stars, maybe more so. Cousy had a very healthy ego. So did Russell. Those egos were a big part of what made them what they were, so it was quite important that Cousy got to make his statement, and that Russell got to make *his* statement, too.

The point is, we all got to make our statements, and this quickly became a very significant factor in the personality of our team. We became like the Mafia after a while. It was no longer just "The Celtics" in our minds. Suddenly it was much more than that. Now it was *La Cosa Nostra*, this "thing" of ours.

That was the way we ended up feeling, which was no surprise, because that was exactly the way Red wanted us to feel.

There was also another important element to Auerbach's approach, beyond establishing *esprit de corps*.

50

As much as he wanted us to be physically well-conditioned, he was even more of a stickler for making sure we were all well-grounded in the fundamentals of the game. He wanted us to become engrossed in the technical aspects of basketball as well as the physical—you know, *Strong mind, strong body!*—and the best way to accomplish that, he felt, was to get us actively involved in the decision-making process so that we'd get to a point where our reactions to game situations would be as automatic as they were correct.

As years went by we began to notice certain similarities in our backgrounds and in the backgrounds of players who came to join us. Most of us had been on winning teams before, many on championship teams, but even the ones no one ever heard of, the ones who hadn't been big-name stars, came from programs where the coaching was sound and where the emphasis was always on *team* basketball. KC Jones certainly wasn't a household name when he came to the Celtics, nor were Sam Jones, Satch Sanders, or even John Havlicek, all of whom played their entire careers in Boston and now have their numbers retired at the Garden.

Red tried to get guys who already knew how to win, who'd already experienced winning, who knew what it was to blend their talents with the talents of others, and, most of all, who understood that success didn't come cheaply, that there was a price that had to be paid. That was one of the things he looked for, a credential he sought out in the selection process. It was one of the things that went into becoming a Celtic. And he always had enough of these guys around so that anyone new who didn't share a similar background fell into line in a hurry.

Yet he never assumed any of us were such complete players that we didn't need to work on the fundamentals, and I mean really basic stuff like how to pass the ball back and forth, how to pass the ball the length of the court, how to dribble full-speed with your right hand *and* your left hand. This is stuff you'd expect high school teams to be working on, even grammar school teams, but not pros. And that's the way most pros feel about it, which is why many coaches at the professional level don't spend a great deal of time on the basics. Then, when their game plans fall apart, they start pointing fingers. You hear them talking about how their players failed to execute properly, when the real problem is that *they* failed to teach them how to execute the intricacies of those plans. The players become the scapegoats for the inadequacies of their coaching and pretty soon no one's happy. You see that happen all the time.

When Carl Braun joined us in 1961, his final season in the league after twelve years with the Knicks, he was amazed to find us going over and over these simple fundamentals in training camp. And this was after we had won three championships in a row, four out of five overall. "I can't believe you guys have been going through this every year," he said. "All we ever did the first two weeks of camp in New York was get acquainted."

But we went back to those basics every year. They were indelibly woven into every one of those drills Red had us do. Sometimes, if he sensed we were getting a bit impatient with all that repetition, he'd tell us he was really doing it for the benefit of the new guys in camp, just to see if they had the same feel for fundamentals we did. Since most of those rookies rarely had a shot at making the team, however, no one misunderstood what was going on. And, despite the occasional grumbling, no one really minded it either.

After all, as he kept reminding us, those camps were designed to produce championships, and once we began piling up all those titles, well, how could you argue with success?

∘ **7** ∘
Welcome to the Big Time!

Now I was ready to play my first game as a Celtic. The kid from Union City had come a long way, baby.

Welcome to the Big Time!

Or so I thought, until we headed to Houlton, Maine.

The year I entered the league it was comprised of teams in Minneapolis, St. Louis, and Fort Wayne; then Rochester, Syracuse, Boston, New York, and Philadelphia. That was it: three little towns in the Midwest, and five towns in the Northeast.

The Celtics were having great difficulty getting any local exposure on television, and it would be a couple of years before we even managed to get all of our road games broadcast on radio. We just weren't popular enough to be profitable at the time.

So we understood that we were not only involved in playing the game; we had to become very much involved in PRing it, too. We came to see ourselves as pioneers, as goodwill ambassadors for pro basketball in New England, as sort of the Pilgrim settlers of the NBA.

Preseason exhibitions were scheduled all over the

map. As fast as gyms were built, we'd get calls to play the dedication games, sometimes even taking on local talent. People weren't coming to games in Boston, so we brought the games to them, traveling highways and byways identified only by their RFD numbers. In time we got to know every legion post and grange hall north of Boston. Restaurants generally would be closed when the games ended, so we'd be invited back to these places for receptions with the locals, who usually fed us stuff like ham and tuna sandwiches.

It doesn't sound like much now, I know, and it's hard to imagine a Magic Johnson or a Larry Bird traipsing through the backwaters of Maine, New Hampshire, and Vermont to get to an endless series of pickup games and cold buffets, but that's what we did, and we had a ball.

It was another aspect of the camaraderie we shared, three or four guys piling into a car and traveling two hundred miles a day, sometimes more, laughing, carrying on, telling stories, doing whatever the hell it is guys do when they're young and on the road together.

The only fights we ever had were over who was going to get stuck in Auerbach's car. Nobody wanted to ride with Red. Not that we didn't enjoy his company—he could be quite entertaining away from the court. It was that we were scared to death of his driving, and that's the truth. If that Chevy convertible of his could have gone 190, he'd have driven it 190, while pumping the pedal for more.

Gene Conley still talks about the night he showed up late and all the cars were filled, except for Red's, which was empty, naturally. Poor Gino had no choice. So he slid in alongside Red and they headed up the New Hampshire turnpike, bound for Maine. They quickly lost the rest of us. It was foggy as hell that night and Red was going 90 miles an hour, following the white line. All of a sudden Conley saw all these lights whizzing by his window, and as they roared back onto the highway he realized the line Red had been following had just taken them in and out of a Howard Johnson's parking lot!

He never said a word. He just sat there tight-lipped and white-knuckled until we caught up with them later that night. Then he came right over to us, still ashen, and said, "Never again, boys. *Never!*"

But back to Houlton, Maine.

I was really looking forward to getting there, to pulling on that Celtics uniform for the first time. Besides, it was a nice day for a ride, late fall, and being a rookie I had no idea where Maine was when we jumped into the cars, let alone Houlton. Going to Houlton is like going to Alaska! You couldn't get there by turnpike, and when we did arrive all I could see were Indians on the streets. I couldn't believe it. After we checked into our motel I decided to go outside and walk around, to see this place for myself, and there was nothing there. It looked like a ghost town the Pony Express had abandoned. So I stood on a corner and kept an eye over my shoulder, half-expecting to be attacked at any moment by a black bear as I waited to make my pro debut that night in an ice-cold Quonset hut.

Welcome indeed to the Big Time, kid.

I continued to live in Worcester that rookie season, but three of the guys whose regular homes were far from Boston—Arnie Risen, Andy Phillip, and Dick Hemric—shared an apartment in Revere, just north of the city, near Logan Airport; and whenever we had an early flight out of town they'd invite me to spend the night with them. Since I didn't relish getting up at five o'clock in the morning to catch a plane at seven, I'd take them up on that offer.

Arnie was about thirty-two at the time, in his twelfth season as a pro, nearing the end of the road as a center and waiting to hand the job over to Russell, who was late in reporting because he was on the Olympic team in Melbourne, Australia. I can still remember him poking me on the shoulder and asking, "Hey, Tommy, how do you like your eggs?" I'd pull the pillow back over my head and mumble, "Any way you want to cook 'em, Arnie."

He loved to cook, so he'd cook everybody's breakfast, no matter how many guys they had staying there, but the deal was always that the guests had to clean up later, which basically meant doing the dishes.

This was all part of the camaraderie, too.

Nobody had money in those days, certainly not enough money to buy a second home for use just during the season, so a lot of guys rented apartments. Quite often two or three of them would rent a place together in order to save some dough. Now when a rookie signs his first contract he runs right out to buy a million-dollar home. That didn't happen in those days. And while the money's obviously nice, it's also taken something very valuable away from the game, something we probably didn't appreciate as much then as we do now because everyone took it for granted. Guys were closer. Teams were more tightly knit. And real friendships were born, the kind of friendships that last a lifetime.

All during those breakfast sessions at Arnie's apartment, all during those rides across the back roads of New England, there'd be constant dialogues going on, usually revolving around basketball, though we shared other parts of our lives as well. It seemed we were always talking about the game, whether it was bitching about Red or about what had happened last night or about what we were going to do when we all got to Syracuse.

I remember hearing Johnny Pesky, a great Red Sox star from the 1940s who works in their organization now, talking about this same thing, about how players back in his era would take an overnight train to Chicago and spend hours together in the parlor car, listening to Ted Williams discuss his theories on hitting. Now, he says, they get off a plane at the airport, grab a cab, and head off to separate rooms at the hotel, after having spent an hour or two together at the most.

Pesky thinks today's players are missing out on a lot of what made sports so special for him, and I think he's right. There's not as much interaction anymore, not as much social interchange of the kind that resulted in bonds as strong as cement.

We rode a lot of trains, too. Some of those towns we played in couldn't be reached by airplane; hell, some of them couldn't be reached by train!

We'd play a game in Rochester, then have to be in Fort Wayne the following night, and it was always a classic example of *You can't get there from here!* There was simply no direct route.

So we'd take a sleeper train out of Rochester, and then at about five in the morning they'd wake us up to make a special stop in the middle of this cornfield located on the outskirts of the nearest town to Fort Wayne. They wouldn't stop in the town, just near it, and just long enough to unload our baggage, which we'd then have to carry as we walked two miles to a place they called the Green Parrot Inn. I'll never forget that name. We'd get to the Green Parrot Inn at about six in the morning, which meant we were now within fifteen miles of our ultimate destination. Then we'd have to bribe some high school kids to drive us the rest of the way.

That was how you got from Rochester to Fort Wayne.

Even before we hit the road to exotic places like Houlton, Maine, however, much of the bloom was gone from the rose. That happened after I got my first peek at our locker room facilities in the fabled Boston Garden.

Actually, *locker room* was a euphemism, since no one really had a locker. You hung your shirt and jacket on a hook. That's what they gave you. A hook. My hook was next to Cousy's hook. And they'd

57

never give you a second hook. Forget that. If you happened to be a clotheshorse who needed additional space, and you yelled about it long enough, they'd eventually relent and bang a nail next to your hook. You knew you had really arrived, that you'd really made it as a Celtic, when they gave you that nail to go along with your hook!

Then all you had to worry about was the shower room. One faucet head usually worked, and sometimes it even had hot water, but the problem was that the drain in the floor was constantly getting clogged. Our toilet—our one john—was two steps up from the shower room, and they even built a little concrete barricade around its base for protection, yet every time the team took showers the water would rise above those steps until our toilet wound up looking like a garbage scow at sea.

Then it would start seeping down to our locker room fifteen feet away, and there we'd be, the famous Boston Celtics, flooded out again!

Oh yeah, kid. Welcome to the Big Time.

But my favorite memory along these lines is of the night we couldn't find a room for Carl Braun in Los Angeles.

Here's a guy who had been All-Pro for a dozen years in New York. He was used to having nothing but the best when it came to accommodations, because the Knicks were always the most financially secure franchise in the league. And again, we had won three championships in a row by the time he joined us in 1961, so I'm sure he must have assumed that we had grown accustomed to *la dolce vita*, too.

We were scheduled to play a Sunday game against the Lakers in LA, and late Saturday night, about midnight, we pulled into the Sheraton West, anxious to hit the pillows. The only problem was, someone had screwed up our reservations. They weren't expecting us until *Sunday* night, and now the place was packed; there just weren't any spare rooms available when we arrived.

Auerbach was hopping up and down, really steamed, and the hotel staff was scurrying around to see what could be done. Eventually, with guys doubling up and using cots, everyone got assigned somewhere, except Carl. He apparently got overlooked in all of the confusion.

"Red," he said, as the rest of us were heading upstairs, "I don't have a room."

So Auerbach put down his bags and went back to the counter to hop around some more, but this time they told him, sorry, there was just nothing they could do, unless, that is, Mr. Braun would be willing to accept some sort of makeshift arrangement.

"Carl," Red says, relaying the information, "they've got nothing. But they tell me they're willing to put a cot in the Grand Ballroom and let you sleep in there tonight. The first room that becomes available in the morning, it's yours, okay? I'm sorry, but it's the best that we can do."

Well, Carl wasn't too pleased about this, but, like Red said, there wasn't much he could do about it, so he took off for the Grand Ballroom, where he stripped down, hopped onto the cot, and went to sleep with all these big chandeliers hanging over his head.

He slept like a rock, right until nine-thirty the next morning, when he heard a lot of people talking and it woke him up. So he tossed off the covers and sat right up in his underwear—smack in the middle of a Communion breakfast!

You know what we told him later, of course.

"Hey, baby, welcome to the Big Time!"

∘ **8** ∘

A Dynasty Is Born

Prior to my arrival and the subsequent addition of Russell, the Celtic teams of Cousy, Sharman, and Macauley were already playing exciting, crowd-pleasing ball. Beginning in 1951–52, when Sharman joined Cousy in the backcourt, they led the league in scoring five years in a row, but their Achilles' heel, weakness on the boards, brought them frustration every spring when the wear and tear of all that running would take its greatest toll, especially on Macauley. The fuel of a fast break is possession of the ball, and they'd always run out of gas at playoff time.

They had enough elements of an accelerated offense to keep their opponents under maximum pressure most of the time, but they just didn't have all the components they needed. Because they didn't have the rebounding ability to limit the opposition to one shot, Cousy became a master at making fast-break baskets *after* the other team had scored. The ball, after going through the net, wouldn't even hit the floor before it would be taken out of bounds, then thrown back to him as far up the court as possible.

The all-time best, in my opinion, at setting up easy baskets for his teammates, Cousy had developed these long, loping hook passes, the kind a quarterback tosses to the guy running for a touchdown, and he'd throw perfect bull's-eyes to teammates already on the fly like wide receivers going through their pass routes.

He had some good ones to throw to, particularly Frank Ramsey, who could catch almost anything. Ramsey was like a second-story man; he'd prowl around until he saw a window open, then sneak in and steal everything out of your apartment and always have his car parked in just the right place for the getaway. He wasn't fast. He wasn't a great shooter. And he was not a great defensive player. But he was *good* at everything, and now, after a year in the service, he was due back soon. The army had stationed him at Fort Knox, guarding the gold—a hell of a place to put a second-story man.

Bill Sharman was one of the best wing people you could ever find for a fast break, and temperamentally he and Cousy were perfect for each other. Bill very seldom went in for layups, unless he was wide open. He'd go into a corner, and if you were guarding him you had to go get him or he'd kill you with his outside shot, which meant he always took one of the defenders away from protecting against the fast break. In addition—and this was missed by a lot of people—Sharman was one of the all-time great defensive players. He was *Ollie North,* baby; one tough sucker when it came to defense. He'd just stick his nose in your face and dog you to death all night. No one ever talks about that. They always say what a great offensive player he was, which was true enough. But Sharman was just as mean at the other end of the court.

Boston had also picked up a guy named Jim Loscutoff a year earlier in the draft. Thanks to Johnny Most, the legendary *Voice* of the Celtics, Loscy came to be known as "Jungle Jim," a name he liked and one that's stayed with him ever since. He sort of lived off the image of being our enforcer, or what hockey would call a goon, which is too bad in a way because there was a lot more to Jim Loscutoff than that. He was a big, tough guy who had some offensive skills, but his primary contribution at the time was strength on the defensive boards. He certainly wasn't the one-dimensional player his reputation suggested. Prior to him, any of the big rebounders the Celtics had—a John Mahnken, a Gabby Harris, a Bob Brannum—were just that: rebounders. As a rookie, Loscy was already demonstrating that he could score as well as rebound if they needed that from him.

Now I came along, and I was one of the missing links. The biggest asset any team can have is speed. When people see a seven-footer walking down the street they think, "Wow, he must be a great basketball player." But that's not necessarily so, even though there are plenty of coaches around who also seem to believe that size is everything. But if you check the most successful teams, the championship teams, the teams that appear to win all the time, you'll find it's the blending of size *and* speed that makes them great. And this is what I offered the Celtics: a big guy who could give them those stable, rock-ribbed ten or more rebounds a game and who still had the potential to replace all the points they lost when they gave up Macauley.

But my basic job, until Russell came, was to help Loscy get the defensive rebounds. With the two of us hitting those boards together we soon began limiting other teams to that one shot, and if they didn't make it, off we'd go! Cousy took a look at me and thought, Wow, here's a kid who can rebound and still get up on the break, so he began to key on me. But unless you're a whippet, which I certainly wasn't, it's extremely difficult to fight the battle of the boards, gain possession for your team, then outrace someone who's standing right beside you. It becomes a sprint upcourt, and all the defender has to do is go straight back. But in order to be a good fast-break forward you're supposed to take a circular route, almost scraping the sideline at midcourt. That creates pressure by imposing decisions on the defense. The further out you're spread, the further out the defense has to spread, and that results in openings you can take in your route to the hoop on the break.

That's what makes James Worthy such a perfect type of player for Los Angeles today. With his blazing speed he can get the rebound for his team, then take a circular route and still outrace his defender to that other basket 94 feet away.

But if there was one aspect of the game I hated it was running, and with Cousy you were expected to go the full 94 feet every time. That's why Red was so insistent that I take off nearly twenty pounds. It wasn't long before I started thinking, "Oh man, what have I gotten myself into here?" In years to come it became a joke that I couldn't run for more than thirty-two minutes a game and, like all humor, it had its strains of truth. Our philosophy never changed: Rush the ball, and never let the defense rest.

Poor old Arnie Risen couldn't wait for Russell to come. He looked like he was going to fall apart each time he ran down the court. I started calling him Mr. Sneeze because every five steps we'd hear him go, *"Achoo! Achoo! Achoo!"* and Jack Nichols, a veteran forward who'd already turned thirty, had a recurring problem with an Achilles' tendon, so every time he tried to run he resembled that Frankenstein monster I felt like on my third day of camp. Dick Hemric was another low-post player who couldn't run. We called him Oak Tree Legs. He had the biggest calves I'd ever seen; his legs went straight down, as if they'd been carved out of a stump. The Boston Celtics was definitely not the kind of basketball team that was going to bring out the best in Dick Hemric. Then there was Togo Palazzi, my friend from Union

City who was two years ahead of me at Holy Cross. Togo was also a forward on that team. We were the same type of player, but he was so into his offense that he'd follow up every shot and forget to go back on defense. That's what hurt him. He wasn't discriminating enough; he didn't know when to rebound from the forward spot and when not to, and opposing teams began to burn him. He was like the pitcher who throws a fastball all the time; it might be overpowering, but once they know it's coming they start hitting home runs. Loscy, despite having a good shot, was not a true fast-break forward, someone who could get out and fill that third lane. And Ramsey hadn't been released from the service yet.

So, for better or worse, I was going to be Cousy's wing man on the break. I offered him what he'd been looking for, that big guy who could rebound and could run.

I became known as the Gunner. That was my image, helped by the nickname "Ack-Ack," as in the sound a Tommy gun makes, which Lennie Koppett of *The New York Times* coined after watching me play the Knicks in an exhibition game for the Milk Fund. But that was my job, and I never got the damn ball unless I was supposed to shoot it. When you're the front man on a break there's only one play to make, and that's to bring it to the hoop. So I did. But I was also our "bailout" guy, the one who'd get the ball whenever a play busted and time was running out, because they knew I could get a shot off. That's where the reputation was born, but the truth is, except for fast breaks, they didn't call a play designed for me more than three times a game.

Yet I scored a ton of points for that team. I did it by creating my own offense, by hitting the offensive glass with moves that were first developed in those back-room games at the St. Joseph's Men's Club. Once Russell came, my job on defense would be to block out my man so that Russell could get the re-

64

bound. Any rebounds that came my way were extras. But on offense, the other team would concentrate so much on blocking out Russell that only one man would be left to guard against me, and I could always get past one man. So I got a lot of tip-ins. That's probably how I scored half of my points. I just loved getting under those boards and beating my man. To me, that was the greatest challenge of all because he had the natural advantage, being between the basket and me. It was up to me to figure a way to get by him, and over the years I devised hundreds of ways to do it.

That was the picture as my rookie season got underway. We were off and flying at the opening gun, and by December 22 we had a record of 16–8, which put us three games in front of the league's defending champs, the Philadelphia Warriors.

Then Bill Russell arrived.

I don't think Cousy knew much about Russell, except what he had heard. I don't think he'd ever seen him play, so he wasn't quite sure what to expect. Of course I damn well knew, after our meeting in that holiday tournament, what this guy was going to mean to us. I knew that here was someone who was going to get us *beaucoup* rebounds. But as for the extent of Russell's impact on the team and the league, I can't say I knew back then what that was going to be. How could anyone have known?

Cousy recognized one thing right away: Russell was going to make us faster. I could feel a surge in my own confidence because of him. Before he showed up I had to stand under the defensive boards and fight my man for the rebound. But his presence changed everything. Russell had an effective rebounding range of eighteen feet. If he was nine feet off to one side of the basket, he could race over to pull down a rebound nine feet off to the *other* side! I saw him do it many times. That's the kind of athletic ability he had. So now all I had to do on defense was *check* my man, just hold him off until he was in no position to challenge for the rebound, then release him and take off. He'd be two steps, four steps, *six* steps behind me as I ran the circular route, leaving him caught in a never-never land: Should he try to catch up with me, or forget me and go straight for the boards?

In effect, Russell was making me play faster than I really was, and he was doing the same thing for Loscy and the others. Energies we once had to expend on defense were now almost totally concentrated on offense. We began crashing the offensive boards with abandon, which meant we were now taking more shots than ever, and our fast break became truly devastating. I could cheat the court and Loscy could cheat the court, because we *knew* Russell would get the rebounds. All we had to do was fly.

Still, I wasn't lifted onto Cloud Nine by all of this. I didn't share the veterans' great sense of thanksgiving. Like Russell I was just a rookie, running around like crazy out there, trying to do everything they wanted me to do. I was a doer; they'd say, "Do this," and I'd do it. I was still learning the system, learning how to run, which was the thing I hated most. So I was much too busy to stand back and try to conceptualize what was going on.

But for Cousy it was different. The Cooz was in heaven! Years later, long after we all had retired, he recalled what was going through his mind back then: "Russ and Heinie couldn't have appreciated what was happening as much as Sharman and I did. They weren't able to draw the comparisons to what had happened in preceding seasons. All of a sudden, after six years of busting our asses and having nothing to show for it, we were top dogs! And you can give Russell the credit for that. He made the game so much easier to play. You could gamble, knowing he was there to cover your mistakes; more important, knowing he had the willingness to cover them. All of a sudden I didn't have to be quite as careful. It wasn't as if every damn pass had to be perfect. There was less pressure now, and that meant my own playmaking instincts could express themselves better. If you have the opportunity to do your own thing, you're going to do it better when everything's loose, when everything's flowing. It was so beautiful, going into a game knowing we could win. It must have been the way Muhammad Ali felt going into the ring, knowing he could just toy with an opponent. That was the kind of confidence we had by the end of that season."

Then Ramsey finally showed up, and now our speed increased even more. He became the original Sixth Man, the prototype of an Auerbach concept in which a player obviously good enough to start is kept on the bench until the first substitutions are made. Most teams lose a bit of effectiveness when one of their starting five sits down, but Ramsey came off our bench with instructions to turn *up* the heat, to step up the tempo, and the effect on the other teams was debilitating. Thanks to Russell, Red could play Frank at forward, though he was only 6'3" and you talk about ack-ack! Ramsey didn't give us any of the slashing inside moves that I had, but he was a lot faster; and when we turned him loose, baby, he'd toss up five shots in the first minute, either popping them in from outside or slipping by his man for easy layups.

Russell's full defensive genius didn't come into its own until his second year. When it did, he would drive guys right out of the league, literally. He turned Neil Johnston, Philadelphia's center and a three-time scoring champion, into a nonentity whenever he played us. Neil couldn't even get off a shot. Russell took opposing centers right out of the game, eliminating all of the old conventional ways of playing the low post with his rebounding. His detractors are always quick to say he couldn't score, which isn't true; he scored plenty of points when it counted. But it's really a moot issue, because when you look at what he did for our offense, and then add to that what he took away from everyone else's, hey, Russell never had to score a single point to be the most dominating player in the history of the game.

We became a truly explosive team that season. While all of the other teams had this metronome inside their heads going *tick-tock, tick-tock,* ours was going *tick! tick! tick!* like a Geiger counter, and now we had the ability to make it work.

That's what Russell did for us. That's the kind of confidence he instilled in us as that season rolled along.

Now only one question remained: How far would it take us?

No one knew. But I think we all had the same feeling, a feeling that something good was about to happen.

○ **9** ○

Champs at Last!

First place was a foregone conclusion long before the regular season ended. Our 44–28 record left us six games ahead of our nearest pursuers, the Syracuse Nats, and now it was time for the acid test; now it was time for the playoffs.

The regular season was one thing; playing three-out-of-five or four-out-of-seven against an opponent who'd have time to prepare and adjust was going to be something entirely different, something I'd never experienced before.

You have to *know* how to do that, especially how to handle your emotions. Russell had been an NCAA champion twice, and earlier that season he had led the Olympic team to a gold medal, so he had a sense of what it was all about. And of course the older guys—Cousy, Sharman, Risen, Nichols, Phillip, even Ramsey and Loscy—had been through this mill before and knew what to expect.

I was the one who really had no point of reference. Yes, I'd been on an NIT champion as a sophomore at Holy Cross, and that was wonderful, but I'd also gone through the trauma of thinking I was a hotshot, only to have my coach put me on the second string after losing to San Francisco. So I guess my personal philosophy about winning the big prize was that if it happened, yes, that would be nice, but the ultimate reward for doing something well was simply to have done it, which goes back again to my empathy with Vincent van Gogh. Championship pressure? If I'd thought about it, it might have gotten to me. But back then the City of Boston wasn't doing handstands over basketball the way it does today. It was far more important to the City of Worcester to have Holy Cross win an NIT title than it was to the City of Boston to have the Celtics capture the NBA crown. That's just the way it was in those days.

So I entered my rookie playoffs totally free of outside pressures, totally unencumbered by the ghosts of the past. My whole approach was *nothing ventured, nothing gained.* I went out and played my ass off, with no regard to the potential consequences, no fear or worry about "losing again." To me it was just, *Hey, man, charge!!!* That was the best of it all: I was free to enjoy it, and I did.

One day during the first round of those playoffs I found a letter addressed to me in our locker room. It was from league headquarters, so I assumed it must have been a fine for getting a technical foul or something like that, but when I opened it a check for $250 fell onto the floor. Russell, whose hook was next to my hook, saw the check and looked over my shoulder as I read the accompanying letter from Commissioner Maurice Podoloff: "I want to officially congratulate you for being selected as the NBA's Rookie of the Year, and this is your remuneration. . . ."

I was still reading it when Russell tapped me on the shoulder and said, "I think you ought to give me half of that check."

I asked him, "Why?"

"Because," he replied, "if I had been here from

the beginning of the year you never would have gotten it.''

Bill Russell. Mister Gracious.

The fact was, even though I was having a hell of a year, there was no question he was going to be a much better player than I was. I knew it, and he knew it, too, and for some reason he was not at all prepared to have a good relationship with me. I don't know if that buildup I got before our meeting in college was still on his mind or what, but buddy-buddies we were not. I recognized he had problems that we probably were not going to be able to work out. I never have had a deep, interlocking relationship with him, though we get along all right today, but I still say now what I said back then: He was the best basketball player I ever saw, and, professionally, there's no one else I ever would have wanted to play with more, no matter what insults he threw my way.

Hey, the insults were part of what made him Bill Russell.

Rookies were expected to carry the bag with the balls as you went from place to place, especially to practices on the road, because the pro ball was different from the college ball and you wanted to be sure you had the right equipment.

So I carried that bag all during the exhibition season and then into the first few months of the regular schedule. Rookie indoctrination, right? I didn't mind. But when Russell showed up in December I figured I'd dump the job on him. Guess again, Tommy. Russell carry the ball bag? *No friggin' way!* So what was I supposed to do, run to Red and ask him to intervene? It just wasn't worth the aggravation, and, besides, I really didn't care; I'd already gotten used to lugging the damn thing around.

It didn't bug me until the next season, when Sam Jones arrived. Now it should have been Sam's turn to carry the bag, but Sam always rode with Russell and there was no damn way the balls were going in Russell's car!

So my reward for being Rookie of the Year was that I got to carry the balls again the following season.

Following a first-round bye, we took three in a row from Syracuse, then advanced into the championship round where we met the St. Louis Hawks. Now everyone could feel the pressure mounting; I still didn't sense it personally, but I certainly was aware of it all around me. Sometimes it was oblique, as in the quietness of a ride to practice, and sometimes it was a bit less subtle, as when Auerbach, after bitching to the refs over the height of our basket before Game 3 in St. Louis, got into a shouting match with Hawks owner Ben Kerner and punched him in the kisser.

But the best illustration of the pressure that was building, pressure that was rooted in frustrations of the past, came in what happened to Bob Cousy and Bill Sharman the day it all boiled down to Game 7 on a Sunday afternoon in Boston Garden.

People talk about that triple-overtime the Celts won from Phoenix in 1976 as perhaps the greatest playoff game of all time. I don't know, perhaps it was. I coached in it, so I certainly can attest to its pulsating drama. But that was a Game 5 situation with the series tied 2–2, which meant neither team was faced with the ultimate pressure of elimination. This showdown we were about to have with the Hawks was for all the marbles, baby; it was winner-take-all! It ended up going into double overtime, and I only wish it had been seen on national TV, because this was truly a game for the ages.

Cousy played the full 58 minutes and shot 2-for-20. Sharman played 48 and went 3-for-20. That's what I mean by being saddled with the ghosts of days gone by: Our Hall of Fame backcourt shot a combined 5-for-40, or 13 percent! Incredible.

The moment that what they were going through really hit me came when Cousy stepped to the line with seconds to go and a chance to ice the game. He had been fouled and awarded two free throws. After he made the first one to tie the score, St. Louis called a timeout. Auerbach, always the positive thinker in a situation like that, was telling us, "When Cooz hits the next one, here's what we're gonna do. First, make sure we don't foul anyone. . . ."

Red reeled off all the things we were supposed to remember, all the possibilities we had to be aware of, except one. No one even considered the possibility the Cooz might miss the shot.

This is no knock on Cousy. He'd been in nine zillion pressure situations over the course of his career, and knew better than any of us how to handle them. That's why we never even talked about what we'd do if he missed. Cousy miss? No way. We were supremely confident he'd make it. But Cooz, like Sharman, wanted to win so badly that day that he tried too hard to play the perfect game, as compared to me, a rookie, who was just trying to go with the flow.

Now we returned to the court as Cooz stepped to the line.

I used to have a little trick for offensive rebounds off missed free throws. What I would do was get my shoulder in front of the guy who had the inside position and let him push me toward the basket. But to be sure I didn't tip him off, I'd wait, looking at the shooter's legs out of the corner of my eye. As soon as I saw the knees go up I'd turn my shoulder and lean, because now this other guy would be watching the ball and wouldn't see what I was doing. After I had positioned myself to let his momentum propel me, I'd start looking for the ball, too.

So Cooz dipped, then his knees straightened out. I knew the ball was in the air and I stuck my shoulder in front of the guy to steal the inside position, then I looked up at the rim to see whether the ball was going through it or not. But there was no ball! I couldn't believe it.

The ball didn't travel six feet after he shot it. That's what I mean by being saddled with the frustrations of the past. All his years of having come so close, only to be denied, came crashing down in this one instant. The emotions he and Sharman were experiencing had welled up to a point where they could no longer play free and easy.

Russell certainly didn't have any of those frustrations. He had 19 points that afternoon. And 32 rebounds.

I had a good day, too: 37 points, 23 rebounds.

But with the clock running down in the second overtime I picked up my sixth personal foul and had to leave the game. That's when my own emotions finally caught up with me. I went to the bench, pulled a towel over my head, and sat there crying. I was whipped. I had played my heart out, and now there was nothing I could do but watch.

That game ended on one of the most spectacular plays I have ever witnessed.

We were ahead, 125–123, and Alex Hannum, the Hawks' player-coach, was standing on the end line next to our basket, getting ready to inbounds the ball with two seconds left. In those days you couldn't call a timeout and then put the ball into play at halfcourt. St. Louis was going to have to cover the full 94 feet in two seconds. Our guys, of course, were all cheating their men, playing them on the top side, the ball side, ready to step in front of any pass. That meant Hannum was going to have to throw what amounted to a baseball pass all the way down the court and have it bounce off their backboard into someone's hands, which would then start the clock.

That's virtually impossible to do. I would defy anyone playing the game today to pull it off successfully, at any time, let alone under the intense pressure that was engulfing Hannum at that moment. But, damn if he didn't do it! The ball ricocheted off the glass and went right into the hands of Bob Pettit, 6'9", their top scorer, just the guy they wanted to see take that final shot. Pettit, who already had 39 points, turned, fired . . . and missed.

We were the new champions.

People lifted me up and carried me around on their shoulders. Red got tossed into the showers. Russell, who had said he wasn't going to shave until we won the title, got his beard shaved off in a locker room ceremony. Everyone was laughing, embracing, pouring beer over someone else's head. Then we all went out to some joint for dinner.

Later Cousy and I rode home to Worcester together and stopped along the way at a club called Bronzo's. Cooz was always kind of a closed guy—he still is—but that night you could see he was absolutely ecstatic. I was, too. So we had a couple more pops together before calling it a night.

And that was it. No boat cruise to Nassau like they have after championships today. When basketball was over it was time to go to your summer job.

I was twenty-two, already thinking about laying down the roots of another career, a career I've been involved with ever since. So I salted away my playoff check for $1,500 and went back to the insurance office I was affiliated with in college.

I was a pretty happy guy that summer, even though I had no idea that the best was yet to come.

° 10 °
Happy Days

It's a lot easier getting to the top than it is staying there. When you're driving toward that first championship, people are much more willing to sublimate themselves, to accept whatever roles are assigned to them, than they are after that initial thirst for success has been quenched, because now they come to the realization that in order for this success to continue they're probably going to have to remain in those lesser roles, quite possibly for a long time.

This was one of the areas where Red was so smart. He'd create a special role for each player, then define it and PR it, making sure that each guy had an identity of his own, or, as I called it, an opportunity for love. He saw to it that everyone's contribution was recognized, and he sold us all on his belief that even a minor contribution on a successful team is far more important than a major contribution on a loser.

Take his Sixth Man concept. It was Frank Ramsey at first, then John Havlicek; but always, by definition, it was someone who, though good enough to start, was asked to remain on the bench while five other guys ran out in the opening introductions to receive a special salute. Red turned that Sixth Man role into such a celebrated aspect of the Celtic Mystique that it still follows Ramsey everywhere he goes today.

Then there was Sam Jones, who joined us the year following that first championship. It was obvious almost immediately that Sam was going to be a great player, yet he spent four seasons sitting on the bench, backing up Sharman, just as KC Jones spent five seasons waiting to step into Cousy's spot.

So the potential for discontent was always there. That's why, whenever writers came to him for quotes to fill up their stories, Auerbach rarely talked about the top scorers or big-name stars. Instead he created love for the guys who came off the bench by raving to the press about their unseen contributions. He did that for years, and I don't think anyone ever picked up on it, except for those guys he was talking about who'd see their names in the papers and know again that they were appreciated.

The exception he made was Russell.

The biggest challenge of all was the one facing Russell and Cousy. If either one of them hadn't been truly interested in winning, we never would have been as successful as we were. Given their fantastic egos, when I think about it today I'm still amazed by how well they worked together. It was as if they realized they needed one another to accomplish what they both had in mind. Cousy, with all that flash and individual brilliance, never won a damn thing until his team controlled the ball. And Russell, who got his kicks from *winning,* period, knew all he had to do was get the ball into Cousy's hands, which was duck soup for him, and the Cooz would take it from there.

But the potential problem here was that everyone in Boston understood what Cousy was doing—the papers long ago had taken to calling him "the Houdini of the Hardwood"—while Russell's genius often went unnoticed. Except for true aficionados, of which there were precious few in Boston in those days, no one really understood this guy's total worth until it began to unfold in all those championships. They didn't even keep statistics on blocked shots in those days. He was like a visionary, so far ahead of his time in the things he was doing that the average fan was missing the entire show.

That's why winning became everything to Russell. Man, that was his statement! They can say all they want about Wilt Chamberlain, Kareem Abdul-Jabbar, or anyone else who ever played the game, pointing to all of their great individual records, but the bottom line is that Russell played on eleven championship teams. That is the ultimate accolade to Bill Russell.

But back when it all began there was a tremendous potential for divisiveness, for resentment, for envy, because here was this white guy everyone loved, getting all of the attention and adulation, while the black guy who turned us into champions was basically ignored by the press, partly because they didn't understand his real value, but also because he was not at all outgoing. He was cynical about people in general, due to experiences he'd had in his own life, and I think the writers were probably a bit afraid of him.

I sat between Cousy's hook and Russell's hook that first year, watching as Cousy, in his own way, invited all of this attention, while Russell, it seemed to me, had an inability to gain it, which just deepened his resentment.

Auerbach saw what was happening. To the press this was just a big black guy—the first potentially great black athlete in Boston—who had no glamour to him at all. Not being well-schooled in the fundamentals of the game and knowing even less about its strategies, these writers could in no way begin to comprehend what Russell was doing, and on top of that he didn't go out of his way to make their jobs any easier.

So Red, knowing what a proud individual Bill was, took it upon himself to become Russell's John the Baptist!

That's exactly what Red was, spreading the word wherever he went, making writers all over the league aware that *He's coming! He's coming! He's coming!* It was as if Vincent van Gogh, who never sold a painting in his life, suddenly had an art dealer come along and purchase all of his works. That's what Auerbach was to Russell: his own personal John the Baptist, a constant reassurance of his greatness. He PR'd him everywhere he went, all the time, much more than he ever did for Cousy, because Cousy didn't need it.

But Cousy was every bit as competitive as Russell. And Auerbach was, too. It was as if somebody had poured the same explosive chemicals into the three of them, because they all had this incredible *need* to win, bar nothing. To the world they appeared invincible, unflappable, incapable of becoming intimidated or unglued. But sometimes things would go wrong and we'd get knocked back onto our heels. We'd fall into a little slump, and this is where their leadership was so outstanding: behind closed doors where no one else was watching except their teammates.

It's easy to stay together when you're winning, but the secret of our team's success was that we never fell apart when we lost. We'd convene team meetings and then open ourselves to the criticism of others, in effect asking our friends, "What do you guys think I can do better?" It was never "You guys aren't getting the ball to me" or "You guys aren't setting enough picks" or anything like that. It was quite the opposite.

We'd all go through it, like a cleansing process. Quite often Cousy would be the first one to stand up. Then Russell would enter into it; he almost seemed to enjoy the process at times. Watching these two bare their souls compelled others to join in, because we trusted each other and, most important, no one was pointing fingers, no one was looking to pin the blame. If anything, everyone was prepared to accept it.

Sometimes we'd ask Red to stay away, which he didn't mind at all. Most coaches want to gather their troops around them and make a speech: "So-and-so, you're not doing this right, so-and-so, you're not doing that right. . . ." Red was different. He wanted his players to have their heads into the game, so he encouraged these closed-door meetings without him. He wasn't afraid something bad was going to happen if he wasn't there. But you've got to be a pretty strong guy yourself to stand aside that way, to acknowledge by your absence that your players were pretty smart, too, and that maybe you didn't have all the answers. Instead of worrying about what might be said behind his back—I can't recall him ever asking what went on in those meetings—Red was always confident we'd emerge even stronger.

And we did.

If someone else criticized us, however, he'd be ready to go to war. The press is always quick to rap you when you hit the skids, and whenever that would happen Red immediately seized the occasion to remind us it was us against the world! He'd point out how writers were always on our bandwagon when things were going well, but that they would be the first ones to jump off at the earliest signs of trouble. Therefore, he told us, we were to trust none of them; they really weren't our friends. The only people we could trust were ourselves, which meant anything that was said in our locker room had damn well better stay in our locker room. Nothing would make him more furious than someone sharing team intimacies with a writer. He would fly into a rage over that: "You want to be buddy-buddy with those guys, huh? Keep it up, and they'll be paying your salary, not us, because you won't be here anymore! Let's get one thing clear, you are part of a team. I don't give a damn who you are or how important you think you are—you're *not* going to air your grievances with the press or be a stoolie for anybody. No way! This is a team and we stick together. Now, have I made myself clear?''

This, of course, just reinforced our sense of *La Cosa Nostra*, just heightened our awareness of this "thing" of ours, and it tended to make us close ranks even tighter whenever we fell into a stretch of bad games. Writers looking for cracks of dissension were not going to get any help from us. We were like Ollie North and John Poindexter, baby; we weren't going to tell Congress anything!

A great example of this occurred during the 1984 playoffs, when the Celtics and Lakers met in the final round. I was doing the games for CBS, and we were in a production meeting where everyone was bemoaning the fact that the Celtics weren't being cooperative. Los Angeles had just croaked Boston by 33 points in Game 3. So I listened for about forty minutes as each one in the room—Dick Stockton, Brent Musburger, cameramen, technicians—took turns expressing great dismay over the truculence of the Boston players. Finally I had to speak up.

"Gentlemen," I said, "you've been covering basketball for a long time now, and you've been talking about this so-called Celtic Mystique for years, how nobody seems to know just what it is. Well, guys, you're looking at it right now. It's smacking you in the face and you don't even realize it."

They all turned to me as if to say, "What the hell are you talking about?"

"It's simple," I went on. "When things go bad, that's when the Celtics close the door, band together, and say you are the enemy! Don't you see, the whole world is their enemy right now. It's them against the world. That's the way it's always been in Boston.

81

They're closing down communications with everyone, not just us. But you watch what happens when they come out to play this next game."

The Celtics won in overtime the following day, then went on from there to nail down the championship.

Another characteristic of Celtics rosters for years was the blending of experience with youth. Our team was a great example of what I call the "push-pull effect," where sometimes older players, with all of their experience, pull the younger players along, and sometimes the younger players, with all of their energy and enthusiasm, push the veterans forward. I think that "push-pull" combination is invaluable to a winning team, if not essential.

It also helps if teams are close off the court.

In the old days this was easier to accomplish because we were forced to have roommates, unlike today when everyone has his own private room. There were just ten players on a team, so what would happen was one pair would wake up and go downstairs for breakfast, and another pair would join them fifteen minutes later, which meant you now had 40 percent of your team getting together over bacon and eggs in the morning. Today, with twelve players on a team, each one having his own room, that same scenario results in *two* players spending extra time together. It's easy to see how the opportunities for off-court camaraderie don't exist the way they used to.

Cousy, though he's shy in a lot of ways, was our captain, the acknowledged leader of our team, and in that role he made it a point to see that we were always having parties or get-togethers at someone's house. When we were on the road it was not at all uncommon to see seven or eight of us heading off to the movies together. It was sort of like a series of marriages in that we made accommodations for one another, going out of our ways to overlook things that otherwise might annoy us.

I'll give you a good illustration. One of my first experiences with Russell as a teammate took place at Madison Square Garden, where we were sitting in the stands watching two other teams play the first half of a doubleheader. My uncle and my cousin were with me and I already had gotten autographs from Cousy and Sharman for the kid, who was about ten at the time. I leaned over toward Russell and asked for his. "If I sign for you," he said, "I'll have to sign for everybody else." I looked at him, as if to say, "Give me a break!" But he was serious. He wouldn't sign. He's always been very adamant about that.

As a result, I became the greatest forger of Russell's signature in the world. Whenever autographed balls were needed for sponsors, charities, Red's friends, or what have you, the guys would say, "Hey, Tommy, put a *Russell* on this one, will you?" It wasn't easy; I'm a righty, and they had to look like a lefty had signed them. My artist's background really came in handy.

I'm sure if Russell had known what I was doing he'd have been mad. I don't know if he ever found out. He might get mad today. But we did it because it was projecting team unity. When balls left that room we wanted everyone's name to be on them; we didn't want the exclusion of one player's name to become a cause célèbre that might result in friction.

So we all agreed to make the ultimate accommodation: forgery.

The only other major potential for friction was in the way Auerbach managed us. Although he was committed to the belief that we all were equals in sharing the team's success—whatever our roles happened to be—there was no way in the world he could treat us all equally.

Here was Russell, this big, skinny black kid whom cops in San Francisco used to pick up and stick into lineups whenever they were doing sweeps, just because he was black. He was a winner, but he sure wasn't an affable guy. He was suspicious of new relationships, especially with whites, and now he had come to a city not known for its hospitality to blacks. So there was no way Red was ever going to yell at Russell.

He wasn't about to yell at Cousy, either. Like Russell, Cousy had enormous pride. You didn't yell at the Cooz.

If you yelled at Sharman he was liable to get up and punch you in the mouth, and Red knew it. If you yelled at Ramsey he took it to heart. If you yelled at Sam he'd brood. If you yelled at KC or Satch or Havlicek, all basically quiet people, they'd be hurt and embarrassed.

And Red *never* yelled at rookies. He'd work them hard, watch them closely, but he'd never go out of his way to criticize them, especially not in front of others. I'll always remember the first exhibition game of Havlicek's second season. Red, after not saying "Boo!" to him in a year, climbed all over him at half time, making him the focus of a locker-room tirade. Havlicek was destroyed. When I saw him come walking onto the court for second-half warmups with his head hanging down, I tossed a ball to him and laughed, saying, "Well, John, welcome to the NBA!"

But there was another reason Red didn't want to yell at these guys. It was the flip side of encouraging them to take active roles in decision making, to be creative, thinking players out there. You can't very well give guys that freedom of expression and then start bitching and hollering at them whenever things go wrong. You had to allow all those personalities and egos free rein, yet control them in such a way that they meshed, and Red was brilliant at that.

Still, he had a need to yell, either to fire up the team or to get some message across in a hurry. So Loscutoff and I became his whipping boys, the ones he'd always scream at when he had a point he wanted someone else to hear. He'd start out, "Okay, Tommy, Loscy, and you other guys, listen up. . . ." Then he'd give the two of us holy hell for whatever it was those other guys weren't doing. We didn't care. We were both kind of happy-go-lucky; and besides that, we understood what he was doing.

Sometimes, though, if I thought it was getting too heavy, I'd go to him and say, "Look Red, ease up, will you? I'm beginning to lose respect. The rookies are stealing my socks!" And he was good about it; he'd stay off my case for a while.

But then he'd always revert to form and chew out my ass again. So one night, after we had run up a huge lead over the other team, when there was nothing he possibly could have been upset about, I sat in the locker room and waited for him to walk in. As soon as he came into view I jumped up in front of the team and said, "Okay, Red, I *didn't* shoot! I *didn't* rebound! I *didn't* block out! What else *didn't* I do?"

Everyone cracked up, including Auerbach.

∘ **11** ∘
The Best Team Ever?

We had a very simple objective at the start of every game: We were going to take more shots than the other team, as many more as we could. So the less time we wasted bringing the ball upcourt, the more shots we'd get, and the easier those shots would probably be because the defense would be caught unprepared.

We were trained to play at a pace other teams didn't like, to extend ourselves 100 percent every minute we were out there. Other coaches preferred to slow the pace so that their players would still be strong at the end of the game if they had to go the full forty-eight minutes. Red's approach was just the opposite: Turn the contest into a physical test of wills!

Even if other teams were able to match us shot for shot, they weren't getting as many good shots as the game wore on because they were being forced to think quicker, shoot quicker, and make decisions quicker, invariably leading to more turnovers than they were accustomed to committing.

We didn't waste a lot of time looking for the perfect

shots, the way other teams did. Our idea was to overwhelm the opposition by the *number* of shots we took; the emphasis was clearly on quantity.

The mathematics of that approach were obvious. If we took 100 shots and made only 40 percent, we'd still have as many points as a team that took 80 shots and made 50 percent. This meant if the other team was trying to limit its number of shots by playing a slower game, it was going to have to shoot a much higher percentage than we did in order to beat us.

We weren't worried about percentages. People look back at those Celtics today and say, "Hey, Cousy shot only 38 percent," but that's a misunderstanding of the way we played.

The constant battle was to find ways to upbeat the tempo and to never allow the other team to slow us down; more important, to never allow them time to catch their breath or to think. This was the essence of Auerbach basketball, the reason Red was so unyielding when it came to his players being in top physical shape.

Most basketball players look at forty-eight minutes the way a marathon runner looks at twenty-six miles: If you don't measure your pace, you're not going to make it. Now all of a sudden here came a team that said: "We're going to *sprint* those twenty-six miles, and we're going to do it by using a relay team!" That's where the role-players came in, because in order to sustain this kind of intense offensive pressure we were going to be needing the strength of all ten of our guys. No other teams went that deep on a regular basis; few went as deep as eight, preferring to go as far as they could with their starting fives. This meant they were playing right into our hands, because if you try to sprint a marathon without a relay team you'll never get past Heartbreak Hill.

The fast break is just a part of tempo basketball, just the mechanics of it. Tempo basketball, the way we played it, is really more of an overall philosophy.

It's as if there are two boxers out there on the court. One is content to jab and dance, jab and dance, while the other one wants to get inside and slug all night, never easing up for a minute, until he finally wears down his opponent with the accumulative toll of all those punishing blows to the body.

That was our style. With Cousy and Russell perfecting what they knew at opposite ends of the floor, allowing us to become more and more assertive all the time, we were simply too much for most teams to withstand. We were the marines, baby! *Charge!* That was us: the leathernecks of the NBA, charging up Pork Chop Hill every night.

Cousy was ordained from above as the best guy in history to run a fast break. He had all the tools at his disposal—including imagination, intuition, and desire —to direct an assault like no one else I've ever seen. He would turn each possession into an immediate weapon, applying pressure the second he got the ball, so that anybody playing against the Celtics had to play 94 feet of defense all night. If just one Celtic got a half-step advantage on his man in the transition, or even a quarter-step, Cousy would spot it. He would take instant advantage of the least little lapse in the other team's concentration. If I had my man beaten by a quarter-step and I was able to maintain that quarter-step lead, I never had to look for Cousy; I'd just take off for the basket and the ball would be waiting for me when I arrived. Bang! Right on the money, every time. That's how good he was.

Since the ball *had* to turn over every twenty-four seconds, there was just no way to stop a fast-break team like ours. We'd score points in clusters, in bursts; great runs of points that would blow a game wide open. We'd wait for the other team to let down, to make a mistake, and then it would be like that little Dutch boy taking his finger out of the dike: *Whoosh!* The ensuing flood would drown him. That's what we would do. They might stay even with us for a period, for a half, maybe even for three-quarters of the game, but we'd be applying this mental and physical pressure all night, especially if the other coach was using only six or seven of his guys, and eventually someone would get tired or there'd be a mechanical breakdown. That's all it would take. Then their dam would burst and everyone would drown.

Other teams were more concerned with precision, with working the ball methodically in order to get a "high percentage" shot. We could play that way, too, but our first instinct was always to rush the ball. We'd score fast-break baskets off *made* free throws! Russell would grab the ball as it went through the net, whip it to Cousy on a quick inbounds, and then we'd shake someone loose for an easy bucket up the court. So even when there was a natural break in the action, we'd still be sprinting, still be forcing the pace. That was the premise: *Never* walk the ball up the floor; always push it!

That approach even helped our defense, making us more willing and inclined to play it. While other coaches were telling their players, "Okay now, we've got to keep them under 100 tonight," Red would be telling us, "Look, if we score 125, all you've got to do is hold *them* to 124. What the hell's so hard about that?" I'll give you an example. One day, during the February vacation week of 1959, we staged a clinic on defense for several thousand high school kids, who then watched us give up 139 points to the Lakers. Russell obviously didn't play that day; he had a sore foot. But with Cousy handing out 28 assists—"spreading the sugar," as he called it—and me scoring 43, we ran up 173 points of our own for a league record that still exists.

Forget for a minute the aesthetics of it. Look instead at the psychology of it. We used to do psychological numbers on people. Cousy loved to do that, and he was great at it.

When you have a three-on-two coming at you, that's

demoralizing enough. In fact, most teams are so content to get a three-on-two advantage that the fourth man won't even bother to run up; he'll hold back and conserve himself. But our fast break was a four-man break. Russell was the only one who wasn't expected to hightail it all night long, which everyone understood because he often had to play the full 48 minutes. The rest of us, however, were constantly engaged in an all-out assault. If I wasn't getting up there fast enough, Red would pull me out and send in a fresh replacement until I got my second wind. He did that with all of us; that's where the "relay team" effect was felt.

So we'd be barreling down on a three-on-two, with the two defenders scurrying, and Cousy would say to himself, "Now is the time!" He wouldn't give the ball to the third man, the open man, the apparent shooter on that break. He'd give it to the *fourth* man, so that it now became a four-on-two, and after this happened once or twice the other team would signal for a timeout and we'd hear them arguing among themselves in their huddle. The coach would be yelling, "Somebody's got to get back there on defense!" And those poor two guys who'd been trying to hold us off would be screaming at their teammates, "What do you expect us to do? Play them *all?*" Meanwhile, we'd be poking each other in the ribs, saying, "Look at that," watching the other coach jab the air with his finger while his players were jawing at one another, all because we were running them down physically and screwing them up emotionally.

That's how much we had refined it, to a point where Cousy could pick his spots. Sometimes he wouldn't pass at all. He used to do this against the Knicks all the time. They weren't a very good team back then, but they'd always play hard as hell against us. So the score would often be close throughout the first quarter. Then, right before the period ended, Cooz would accelerate the attack, turn it up a notch, and when he finally had three of us breaking in at once he'd just step back and toss in a running right-hander off the wrong foot! You could almost see them throwing up their hands at that point, as if to say, "We ain't never gonna beat these guys!"

Okay, maybe that sounds arrogant; we certainly were accused of arrogance in those days. But I don't think it was arrogance as much as it was supreme confidence in our abilities, supreme confidence in one another. As Muhammad Ali once told the late Red Smith, after Red had suggested to him that his poetic predictions weren't very gracious, "It ain't braggin' if you can do it."

Like Ali, we could do it.

Teams would walk onto the court for the opening tap all psyched up to play us, ready to give us a good go, and they'd hang in there with us for a while. But when you keep taking eighteen seconds, twenty seconds, to carefully set up what you believe to be your highest-percentage shot and then throw yourself completely into a defense that's constantly under attack, and you keep doing this over and over, eventually someone gets mentally fatigued, even before he gets physically wiped out. Cousy was like a ferret whenever that happened. He'd spot it right away, and that's when he'd send a thirty-foot bullet pass right by the player who was pooped. The effect was devastating.

Opposing players began describing the experience in terms of having this huge Green Wave bearing down on them all night long, threatening to wash them all overboard at any given moment.

Hell, that was no wave. That was a damn typhoon!

And that was Cousy; not only a magician, going behind his back and between his legs to make those beautiful passes, but also a master psychologist. He just loved playing mind games on people, the way Larry Bird does now. Magic Johnson's been at it so long that he's becoming a bit of a psychologist, too.

He's clearly one of the all-time great middle men on a fast break, yet Magic doesn't even comprehend what Cousy knew about destroying the will of the other team to beat you.

People ask me today who I'd put into my all-time backcourt from those days, assuming the answer will be Oscar Robertson and Jerry West. I say it makes no difference; I'll gladly take either one of those two, but the other guard has to be Cousy. They think I'm nuts, so they start throwing scoring stats at me, the way they do whenever they hope to make the case that Wilt Chamberlain was better than Russell. And my answer is always the same: "Yeah, stats are great, but tell me, who won all the titles?" Then they'll tell me Cousy never won a thing until Russell came along, which is true enough. But Jerry never won a thing until he teamed up with Wilt, and Oscar never won a thing until he played alongside Kareem Abdul-Jabbar.

The fact is, no one's ever won a thing in the NBA without a quality big man in the middle. Cousy just happened to have the good fortune to play with the best big man of them all.

Russell was like a Cézanne on defense, a craftsman who perceived his art form in a unique way that led to a whole new school of thought. Cézanne, the great French postimpressionist, did it with geometric forms. Russell did it with timing, with great leaping ability, with blocked shots, and, like Cousy, with a particular delight in the psychology of it all.

Prior to Russell, everyone was involved essentially with guarding his own man. But then Bill introduced us to what he called a "help defense," or what some of our guys began calling the "funnel defense," in which everyone was free to gamble a bit, to overplay his man on the outside, driving all of that traffic inside or down the middle, where Russell had set up a road block.

I called it the "Venus's-Flytrap Defense." You invite the man you're guarding into a specific area of the court. It's a very appealing area, one that appears to be wide open, one that looks to a shooter's eyes like the nectar of the gods. But then as soon as you get him inside that area it closes tight, chews him up, and spits him out. That's what Russell did. That's what Russell was: the ultimate Venus's-Flytrap.

Sam Jones joined us my second year, followed by KC Jones a year later, and now we had added yet another dimension to those problems we were already creating around the league. Until their arrivals, even with Russell on hand to help, our defense had been more or less passive. Sharman and Cousy didn't have great quickness. But now Red began sending "the Jones Boys" out there together as an Attack Team, and they became the final ingredient that made us truly awesome.

Other teams, already under intense physical pressure on defense and trying to cope with our break, suddenly found themselves being hawked all over the court on offense. Sam and KC never gave them an inch of daylight, gambling each step of the way, lunging at the ball every chance they got, knowing Russell was waiting to back them up if anything went wrong.

We all gambled. We all cheated the court and took chances. Russell made us all more aggressive, the way Cousy made us all faster. And Auerbach made sure we all stayed hungry.

Bring on the world! That's how we felt. As Satch Sanders once so aptly put it, "We were just kickin' ass and takin' names out there." He was right. And that went on for years.

So, were we the best team ever? I don't know. I'd say eight championships in a row certainly makes a compelling case.

But I will tell you this: We were the hardest team of all time to beat. And until someone comes up with a better guideline for measuring greatness, that one's good enough for me.

◦ 12 ◦
Swan Song

They say all good things must come to an end, and no one knows that better than the athlete whose career has finally come to its sunset.

An athlete is like a beautiful woman, maybe a movie star, who looks into the mirror one day, sees a wrinkle, and suddenly realizes she's no longer young. In his case, maybe he's just lost a step or two, or maybe he's even lost his job, and now all of a sudden his whole perception of himself changes. He thinks, "It can't be me," and maybe he starts to point fingers, because up to that point his entire life has been based on his body's ability to do what he wants it to do. And now that it can't quite do that anymore . . . well, that can do an awful job on his psyche.

My sunset came in 1965 after nine seasons with the Celtics. I was thirty. I could have hung around longer if I'd wanted to; the decision to leave was mine.

The Celtics, back in those days before free agency, were unusually loyal to their veterans. When it became obvious that a Sam Jones, for instance, was ready to play full time, they didn't toss a Bill Sharman out the back door. Other managements would have been tempted to shop him around while he still had name value, figuring they knew more about his *real* worth than anyone else did and hoping they might get a younger player with a longer future in return. The Celtics didn't operate that way. That's why a Jack Nichols, who could hardly run when I arrived, was kept an extra year or two. They thought he might know a thing or two he could teach a kid like me, which he did.

Those loyalties meant a lot to veterans. You weren't, for instance, afraid to buy a house, thinking you might get dumped when you weren't expecting it. That didn't happen in Boston. After trading Ed Macauley to St. Louis for the draft rights to Russell in 1956, it would be ten years before Red traded away another established Celtic; that was in 1966, when he traded Mel Counts for Bailey Howell. In my entire career, I never saw a teammate of mine traded away. That's incredible.

It wasn't at all like playing for, say, the Pistons, whose owner, Fred Zollner, let his girlfriend talk him into trading away George Yardley—a great player, the first one in NBA history to score two thousand points in a season—because she said bald guys didn't make good matinee idols.

Those loyalties were not only appreciated in Boston, they were also repaid in many ways.

Red's former players were always calling him with tips about prospects they'd seen. There was no sophisticated scouting in those days, so you relied heavily on the advice of people you trusted. It was Fat Freddy Scolari, living in San Francisco, who first alerted Red to Russell. It was Bones McKinney, living in North Carolina, who first tipped him off about Sam Jones.

I helped him select a player, too. I helped him select my own replacement, Don Nelson.

Red knew I was thinking of packing it in, so he

asked me what I thought of different players in the league. "This kid Nelson," I told him, "is slow, but he can shoot the hell out of the ball. He's so slow I thought I'd be able to drive right around him, but the sucker can play defense, and he's a good rebounder. He's very tough to score on. You just can't get in there, he blocks out very well. He's one of the few people in this league who always seems to do a number on me. I'd get him."

So Red got him, and Nelson played eleven seasons in Boston.

That's the way we operated.

If I had wanted a "Tommy Heinsohn Day" I could have had one. Cousy had a Day. Havlicek had one. Loscy had one. A lot of the guys had them. I could have arranged to walk away like that, with one last loud ovation ringing in my ears. But that wasn't me. I was never into that stuff.

Sure, at one time, back in the beginning, I was like everyone else: I wanted to be All-American, I wanted to be All-Pro, I wanted to be a *star!* Then one night we played an exhibition against the Lakers in Seattle, and I was super, if I do say so. I had 40 or so points, 20 or so rebounds; in effect, I won the game for us. So when I came downstairs for breakfast the following morning I reached for the papers to read about myself. There was this nice two-page spread saying how Elgin did this, and Jerry did that, and Russ, Cooz, Sharman, blah, blah, blah. On and on it went. Then I got to the last paragraph. It read: "Tommy Heinsohn added 40 points and 20 rebounds." I closed the paper, looked at Gene Conley, my roommate, and said, "Gino, babe, I don't think I'm ever gonna be a star!"

So I stopped worrying about it and looked for other reasons to play. I wasn't in it for the glory. After a while that almost became repugnant to me. What intrigued me was the physical challenge of basketball, the intellectual stimulation, the creative excitement.

And that's why I was quitting. I had reached a point where I didn't think I was going to be a part of that anymore.

I was considered to be a rough, tough, grumpy, complaining, miserable, bitchy, mean player—*and I was an artist!* I am not like that in other things that I do . . . I hope.

But basketball was my turf, my statement, and when the game was on, that was my true personality. People were always working on my temper, on my inability to control it. But the guy I was getting mad at usually was myself. Look at John McEnroe. Half of the things he fusses about are things he knows he's doing wrong, so he gets mad at himself: *Why am I screwing this up after all those hours of practice, after all the time I've worked on this move? Now, when I really need it, I can't get the damn thing to go right!* People interpret this to mean he's a weirdo. But I don't. I understand his anger.

What you've got to do, what I had to do, is try to control that anger, try to give yourself the benefit of the doubt more often so that you can turn that energy into something positive. This anger all stems from some neurotic drive most players have, some neurotic need to be perfect. That's what drives them to greatness, that unwillingness to accept or tolerate imperfections. They don't cast them off easily; instead, they get mad at themselves. That's why the battle becomes one of harnessing these emotions so that they don't take away from the energy of the actual competition. And that's why teammates were always trying to get me to control my temper, to stop getting mad at myself or at the referees. I never truly mastered it. If someone belted me, man, I was going to belt him back *twice,* because that was *my* statement: You're not going to intimidate me, pal. That's not the way you're going to beat me!

Ask Wilt Chamberlain.

Wilt was a monster. Thank God he had a good

personality. He was a much milder-mannered guy than Russell, but he could be provoked on occasion, and one of those occasions occurred during the playoffs of 1960, when we went six games with his Philadelphia Warriors before eliminating them in the Eastern finals.

Red had devised this play in which I was to get into Chamberlain's way each time Philly shot a free throw, so that Russell could break free for easy baskets down the other end of the court while Wilt was tangled up with me. Once he caught on to what I was doing he got really mad and said, "I'm going to knock you onto your ass if you try that again." Naturally, I had an answer for him. "Yeah," I replied, "you and your mother!"

Well, sure enough, he was true to his word. When I did it again he knocked me onto my ass, and now he was coming to finish the job, to really clean my clock. He threw a punch while I was getting up off the floor, just as Tom Gola happened to walk between us. The punch popped Gola in the back of the head by mistake and Wilt busted his hand. Now I was on my feet, and I chopped him a couple of times—but he didn't even know I was hitting him! He just held his hand, because it hurt.

So now we came back to Boston to resume the series, and Wilt was playing with the broken hand. One of our other strategies had been to deny him the ball as much as possible by jumping all over the passer, making it difficult to get a pass in to him. Russell would sort of three-quarter him on defense; that is, position himself to pick off the pass before Wilt got it. But if it went over Russell's head, then the weak-side forward was supposed to rush over and foul Wilt deliberately. We used to use up all of our forwards' fouls that way, helping Russell defend against him, because everyone knew Wilt couldn't shoot free throws.

So now we were working this defense and everything was going all right until a pass flew over Russell's head. I came rushing in from the weak side, but Wilt had already got the ball and was heading for the hoop. There was nothing I could do at this point except to try punching the ball loose.

That's what I did, but I ended up punching his broken hand instead, and I heard this loud groan: "Ooooo-owwww!"

They called a foul on me, and as we were all heading for the line Wilt was still moaning and I was thinking to myself, "Oh boy, what's going to happen now?" He looked at me while he was waiting for the ball, and I looked back at him, as if to say, "Do you want to make something of it?" It had now become a stare-down contest, and I was throwing as much bravado at him as I could muster. He never took his eyes off me until he got the ball, but I had a sense he was telling himself, "This crazy German's nuts. I'd better let it pass."

We never had another confrontation in all the years I played. It had been a mind game, that's all; and to a degree I think I actually intimidated him, even though we both knew he could have killed me with his bare hands.

That's what made the game for me. I lived for moments like those. I loved them.

Now they were over and I knew it. I'd given all I had to give. My body was telling me it was time to go.

So I went to Red before the playoffs and told him I wasn't coming back, just so he'd know as he planned for the draft. And I also told him I wanted no "Night," no big fanfare, no special attention at all, although the news leaked out eventually. I wanted to leave on my own terms. I told him that was important to me, and he agreed.

We went on to beat the Lakers for our seventh consecutive championship, the eighth of my nine-year career. The only one we missed was in 1958, when

Russell wrecked his ankle trying to block a shot in Game 3 against St. Louis. But even after losing him we took the Hawks to 6, with me trying to stop the great Bob Pettit. And we *almost* took them to 7; Pettit had to score 50 for them to beat us 110—109 in that final game, after which Cousy captured the moment by yelling across the locker room, "Damn it, Tommy, if you had held him to 49 we might have won."

Everyone laughed.

That's what it had been for nine years: A barrel of laughs.

Even my final game was a laugher. We opened the fourth quarter by scoring 20 points in a row to blow the Lakers right out of the Garden. Now, as the clock was winding down, I was sitting on the bench and I could hear people yelling for Red to send me out there. He came over and asked if I wanted to go in one last time. I told him thanks, but no. I played basketball to be a part of it; I didn't want to leave with a token appearance.

I wanted to leave *my* way, and I did.

° 13 °

The Love Ache

The public sees an athlete as a guy who, in a very short period of time, conquers all adversity. He's a victor. He's someone who finds a way to solve all of life's problems in 48 minutes, night after night, city after city. No matter what his enemies do to him, somehow he wins. That's what makes him a hero.

Johnny Most, the Voice of the Celtics, has it right: It is indeed the White Hats versus the Black Hats. That's what it is to people who watch. It's precisely the drama he's been portraying for thirty-five years: Every Celtic is a good guy, and all the other guys are bad guys; unless, of course, they happen to become Celtics, at which point, somehow, they undergo a miraculous transformation as they cross the River Charles and are instantly baptized into Celtic-hood.

It's just like the theater, only here the actors are ballplayers. That's really what ballplayers are: They're actors in a constant mini-drama, portraying roles that come to be identified with them. Some are villains. Cousy was the butler, handing out all those assists. He's remembered today for the imagination he brought to his role. All the great ones—Bird, Magic, Michael, Dr. J, Gordie Howe, Bobby Orr, Wayne Gretzky—do that. After they've mastered all the mechanics their roles demand, they then add their own special touches of emotion and creativity, raising those roles to levels of excellence that elevate them far above the crowd.

No matter how well you play your part, though, it's still just that; it's only a part, a role you have in a drama. It's not who you really are. And when the curtain comes down, when the play is over, you find out you're just a person like everyone else. Being very human may be very much at odds with the role you portray. Basketball's only a game. Life is a whole lot different. You can *fail* out there, baby, for reasons that are very legitimate. The learned skills of living are much more complicated than the learned skills of playing, and at any given moment in your life you're apt to find yourself 20 points down heading into the second quarter.

There are people, however, who want to believe that you really are the master of every situation, even off the court. The media add to this misconception by attempting to extend that role into your personal life. As Satch Sanders once said, "They write that an athlete is dedicated, but what does dedicated really mean? Fans assume it means he's a wonderful parent, a wonderful citizen, a pillar of the community, when all it probably means is that he keeps his body in shape and gets to practices on time."

They want you to be who they think you are. You're like the beautiful girl at the discotheque. Guys conjure up in their minds an image of how sophisticated and sharp you must be, and the result is that even the ones with great gifts of gab get tongue-tied attempting to strike up a conversation with you.

It's the same way with ballplayers. Back in the early days of my career my wife had a friend who used to go to all the games with us. Her husband often came along, too. He was a mechanic in a factory and later ended up the general manager of a big manufacturing company. He certainly was a successful guy, an interesting guy, yet all he ever wanted to talk about with me was basketball. Whenever I'd try to talk about him, he'd back off. And this is what happens all the time. You want to have a relationship with someone, but if that someone won't participate in it, won't contribute to it, the relationship goes nowhere.

I remember going to a cocktail party up on Beacon Hill, where all the old Boston Brahmins live. This was my first year with the Celtics, before they were a household name. I was mingling, trying to be friendly, when a woman and her husband came up and asked what I did for a living. I told her I played for the Celtics. She asked, "Who are they?" As soon as I told her they were a basketball team the conversation was over. They didn't know anything about basketball and their assumption, I guess, was that I wouldn't know about anything else. That hurt. It was like saying all I was good for was basketball.

But sometimes it's worse when people do know who you are, when they watch you and read about you all the time. How often do you get to watch someone doing his job every day? You don't get to watch the doctor in the operating room, the teacher in the classroom, the mechanic in the garage. That's why, when you do get to meet a doctor, for instance, it's nice to talk about what he does. But if all he wants to talk about is what *you* do, if the sucker doesn't open up and share what he does, too, then he's using you, man; you're being raped. It happens a lot, and the athlete walks away from these encounters asking himself, "Why can't I have a conversation with this guy?" He thinks it's *his* fault, and it's not.

In order for you to share in the benefit of a social relationship with people, they have to ante up, too. If they don't, maybe it's because they feel inadequate, or maybe they're intimidated by your celebrity. Whatever the reason, it's as if they can't bring themselves to have a rapport with you on any level other than that of the image they've created for you.

In time you come to the realization that you are not responsible in any way, shape, or form for what strangers think about you, because they'll have already formed their opinions. Some will be in your corner; they'll think you're terrific, and groove on you for no apparent reason, but it won't make you feel particularly good because you'll know there's no basis for their affection. Then some will hate you for reasons that are just as superficial. And no matter what you do it's unlikely you're going to change the opinion of either group because they have no rationales for their positions. Somewhere in between is a third group that will evaluate you on what you did that day; some days you'll be seen by them as good, and some days you'll be regarded as bad. When this happens often enough there's a danger of letting yourself get locked into that image, too. This is particularly dangerous for that athlete who lacks the self-confidence to insist on being who he really is, and tries instead to fulfill an image for everyone he meets.

That's not only a fraudulent way to find friendship, it's also very frustrating, because you know the truth. Yes, you've mastered the skills of your game, but you also know you haven't mastered anything else, and eventually, you keep reminding yourself, that truth is going to be revealed. It's not a pleasant thought to contemplate at all.

When I left basketball I went into the insurance business full time. I was one of the few people able to combine an active career in sports with a professional career on the outside. All through my years with the Celtics I was among the sales leaders in my company's Worcester office, making more money as a salesman for State Mutual of America than I was as a forward for the world champions. Then, when I came to the end of my playing days, I was asked by the home office if I wanted to get into management, to become a general agent, which is sort of like being president of your own little business. I took the tests, did well, and then trained under a general agent who was about to retire and whose office I'd be inheriting. In the three years I was there we went from a $2 million agency to a $10 million agency; and yet, when I was devoting just 20 percent of my time to selling, I was still among the company's top five salesmen. Today I'm a CLU, a Charter Life Underwriter, which is the insurance industry's equivalent of a CPA degree.

People are often surprised to learn that about me, just as they're often surprised to learn I'm an artist who's had several shows. Public perceptions are sometimes very different from realities.

One of the things you discover in the insurance industry is that a great number of business executives who've been forced to retire at sixty-five die within six months. It's a statistical fact. Why? Because their identities were so wrapped up in what they did, in who they were, that once all of this was taken away from them they had a very difficult time adjusting; they couldn't find another reason to live. Believe me, that's a very tough number.

Ballplayers go through the same kind of crises, only they go through them at twenty-eight, thirty, or thirty-two, with whole lifetimes still ahead of them. They at least have the resiliency of youth to fall back on, along with some lessons they should have learned in sports, namely, that you don't always win, and that hard work and dedication are the ways to get you from where you are to where you want to be.

Yet, for some, retirement is still sheer terror.

It requires a great deal of humility, because after having been so successful at one thing, you've got to change gears and learn something else, something you're not very good at, something at which you're probably going to make a lot of mistakes. People as successful as athletes have been don't like making mistakes, especially when other people are watching; their egos are too large and too fragile for that.

If you've been trained all your life to find acceptance through doing something well, you find failure of any kind difficult to accept, because failure can be translated as rejection. I've known ballplayers who couldn't accept success, because if they accepted success they knew they would also have to accept criticism when they failed, and they were unwilling to do that. So they publicly came out looking like very humble people when, in effect, what they really were was afraid of failure.

When I first got into the management end of insurance, I started recruiting athletes for our company, assuming they'd be naturals because they were highly motivated people who came from backgrounds of achieving goals. But it didn't work out that way. When we tested them we discovered that a vast majority had very low self-images. That might have surprised their fans, who really want to believe the myths. But it didn't surprise me, because I understand the realities. That doesn't mean I didn't find it sad.

Some athletes make so much money they'll never have to work again, never have to expose themselves to the humiliation of failing at something else. But retirement has some horrors in store for them, too.

The dark side of sports is that, from the earliest stages, the athlete is conditioned to relating his success in the game to his acceptance as a person. The first time I became aware of that was back in grammar school, when the older kids invited me to play on the varsity court. That was acceptance! That made me a special kid. It made me different from all the other kids. And when that first happens to you, when people first start treating you with deference and respect, you tell yourself: "Wow, I want more of this! This is great."

That's when it starts, out there on the playgrounds, out there in the schoolyards, especially in the inner cities where there aren't too many adults around, where the battle is for turf—who plays and who doesn't play; who's going to get laughed at and who's going to be taken seriously. The kid who is looking to establish an identity discovers that the answer lies in acceptance, and acceptance comes quickest to those who excel at games.

That's where the obsession begins.

Does an obsession motivate some athletes to be as great as they are? Yes. But in order for there to be an obsession, which by definition is an abnormal preoccupation with something, there has to be, correspondingly, as deep a need; a need that the obsession is offsetting. I believe the need that motivates most great athletes is some form of love deprivation.

I call it the Love Ache.

I used to tell people I thought Bill Russell had a neurotic need to win. They'd laugh, but I wasn't trying to be funny. You talk about being obsessed! There are very few men in everyday America who'd be willing to put into their jobs what Russell put into his. I've read Russell's books. This is a guy who's been in personal turmoil much of his life, who's been screwed more than once by society. He always denied that the adulation meant anything to him, even to the point of refusing to participate in the retiring of his number at Boston Garden and refusing to attend his own induction into the Hall of Fame. I never believed him. I think he not only liked the adulation; I think that's why he was in the game. And I think the greatest denial of all is that he won't even admit that to himself.

Cousy had a speech impediment. Ramsey had a super-successful father, a real tough dude. I don't know this to be a fact, but my guess has always been that all of these guys were driven by a need for love, for acceptance, for dramatic reassurance in their own minds of their own worth, and they found that reassurance through their excellence in sports.

Their love ache was dulled by winning, by being acclaimed as winners, just as mine was. Hell, I was the neighborhood Nazi, remember? I damn well had a need for love.

When I looked at Dave Cowens years later I saw traces of that. Cowens had a ferocity about him, a burning drive he picked up somewhere in his life. I know he had great respect for his brother, who became a doctor. David considered that to be much more important than basketball in the overall scheme of things. Maybe that's why he was always looking for something else to get involved with, some other cause to take up, some other fight to win, even while he was leading the Celtics to titles. He'd go out of his way to dismiss what he was doing on the court as relatively unimportant. "There are no heroes here," he'd tell writers, over and over again. "We're just basketball players, doing what we get paid to do. If you want to talk to heroes, go talk to soldiers." When he walked away from the team for thirty games in the 1976–77 season, emotionally drained, he tried being a cab driver. I don't think Dave really knew what *normal* was, and that bothered him; he just knew the answer wasn't basketball.

Larry Bird? I don't know what drives that guy, but I'd love to talk with him about it sometime. He's as compelled, as driven, as obsessed as any great athlete I've ever seen. He's up there with Cousy and Russell when it comes to brooking no reason for not succeeding. There's got to be some of this love ache in him.

It's obsession. That's what it is. But it's *focus,* too. The great ballplayers have always been the ones who could focus their emotions like a laser beam, burning away their opponents with intensity. Jerry West. Elgin Baylor. Magic Johnson. John Havlicek was like that—in some ways he was the most focused athlete I ever met. From the day he showed up as a rookie until he retired sixteen years later, his approach and attitude never changed. Then again, you could not talk with John Havlicek about the war in Vietnam. It was as though the NBA was his world at the moment, and everything else was excluded. As long as he played, I never knew of John to be involved in anything but basketball. He was truly a nine-to-five guy: He got married, had kids, and led what society would call a normal existence. And he seemed happy. I cannot tell you what motivated him to greatness; I don't know if he knows. I doubt he's even thought about it yet.

The problem with sports is that all careers are terminal, so if you're used to getting your acceptance from what you do, rather than getting it from who you are, you are on a collision course with a major emptiness in your life.

First, there's the absence of instant gratification when you retire. Psychologists are fond of describing "peak experiences," those special moments of triumph or happiness we remember forever, but sports offer something even better: When you win a championship, it's the *ultimate* experience! Everything you are, everything you've worked and trained for, everything you've hungered for—all of your emotions, your intelligence, your courage, your skills, your techniques, your whole personhood—all of this is poured out at once, and, baby, when it clicks, when it all comes together in front of your eyes and you see the results immediately, when you feel the results flowing all through your body . . . that's the ultimate thrill, the ultimate acceptance. You're a champion! And the euphoria of that moment lifts you above all normal feelings you've ever known. Moreover, you're not the only one who's feeling it. You look around and see the other guys on your team feeling it, too. You've done it together, and now you're savoring it together, and for the rest of your lives you're all going to share a very special bond, a closeness you'll experience all over again whenever and wherever you meet. It's beautiful.

Where do you find that in the outside world? Even if you find success out there, it's never the same. If you sell a ten-million-dollar life insurance policy, you first have to check out the situation, then refine it, make some phone calls, talk to the lawyers, see the accountants; then the guy has to be examined. It's a long process. It might take six months. The gratification is there, but the full impact is diluted by the time the deal is done. It never hits you all at once the way it does when that final horn sounds and the celebration starts.

That part of your life is over. It was like a love affair while it lasted. Call it admiration, call it adulation, call it acceptance; whatever it was, it filled a need. It dulled the love ache. From that first home run in Little League, when all of the other parents cheered; from the night you came home and told your dad you'd been picked for the traveling team in youth hockey; from the time you made that first move on the court that had the other guys going, "Wow, dig him"—from all of those moments, whichever of them happened to have been yours, your identity in the eyes of the world and your image of yourself have been linked to this thing you do so well.

I am a basketball player!

Correction. You *were* a basketball player.

And what hurts you now is the slow realization that this wasn't love at all, because it wasn't based on reality. They weren't cheering you; they were just cheering what you did. And now that someone else is doing it, now that someone else is getting all of their attention and all of their cheers, you tell yourself, "Well, I guess that wasn't the answer." And it's very easy to feel ripped off at that moment, no matter how much dough you've salted away. You'd be surprised if you knew how many of your onetime favorites are feeling that way today.

I had my neuroses, too. When I said art and basketball were my "friends" as a boy I was telling the truth, and it would be years before I realized how psychologically damaging those childhood experiences were. I'm still learning to deal with them today.

Two of the things I've been carrying around with me ever since I was a kid are a dramatic, neurotic need for love and a learned pattern of behavior for how to get that love on a personal basis.

I've emulated my mother. She had a very unfortunate childhood. Her mother died young, and her father later married a woman who didn't want my mother living with them, so she was brought up by a succession of aunts and learned to get her love by helping them. There's a book by Robin Norwood called *Women Who Love Too Much* (J. P. Tarcher, 1985) that I found fascinating. It not only described my mother; it described traits I developed, too, growing up without friends and watching her continue to care for those aunts long after she and my father had set up a home of their own.

I'm sure that's one of the reasons I was attracted to the insurance business. You get to know people on a very intimate basis when you're talking about the life and death of loved ones. That's getting right down to the nitty-gritty, which I liked; it put me in a position to help people.

And believe it or not, that's why I went back to basketball five years later, this time as a coach. It wasn't the money that brought me back. Hardly. It cost me money to go back.

I went back because I was going to *help* the Boston Celtics.

◦ **14** ◦

Return to Battle

Six months after I retired as a player, Auerbach asked me to succeed him as coach.

It was October 1965. Red had just announced, a year ahead of time, that this was going to be his final year on the bench. As he explained to the writers: "I'm announcing it now so that no one can ever say I quit while I was ahead. I'm telling everyone right now— Los Angeles, Philadelphia, everyone—that this will be my last season. You've got one more shot at Auerbach!"

Eight months later he won it all again, his Last Hurrah.

But now he had asked me to meet him in Philadelphia, where he offered me the chance to be his successor. I turned him down, and when he asked why, I gave him a truthful answer: "Because," I said, "I don't think I could handle Russell."

We began discussing other possible candidates, and after we had tossed around several names I said to him, "Want to know something, Red? I think you ought to make Russell the coach. He's got so damn

112

much pride in himself, and this would just add to it, being the first black pro head coach in history. He'd get more out of himself these next few years than anyone else could.''

Red gave the job to Russell that spring, and in the three years Bill was player-coach the Celtics won two championships. Then he quit, supposedly in the summer of 1969. At least that's when the news broke, in a *Sports Illustrated* article he wrote titled "I'm Not Involved Anymore." It caught most people by surprise, but not me. I knew he was hanging them up right after they beat the Lakers in Game 7. It ended up a two-point decision, 108–106, but in the third period, when the Celts ran up a 15-point lead, Chamberlain took himself out of the lineup, complaining of a sore knee. Russell called him "a quitter" after the game. That's when I knew he wasn't coming back. Russell never would have put the rap on Wilt if he intended to play him again; he never would have given him that psychological tool. So when he called him a quitter I knew what it meant: It meant he was taking his final shot at the guy.

I stepped in when Russell stepped out.

Some people laughed when I got the job. They thought I was a buffoon. Leigh Montville, a *Boston Globe* columnist, captured it pretty well when he wrote: "Tommy Heinsohn is forever the twenty-foot hook shooter. The comedian. The kid forever in the back of the room, making funny noises while the teacher is declining Latin words on the blackboard. He is hard to take seriously. . . ."

It was an image Auerbach didn't help very much by occasionally sitting near the bench. Everybody thought he was giving me hand signals, telling me what to do next.

I'm not a dummy, okay? Red took me for granted in a lot of ways over the years, especially with that "whipping boy" stuff, yet he and I also shared a special relationship, sort of a mutual admiration society. He knew I was an intelligent guy, a businessman, and he knew my thinking on basketball was a lot like his own. Hell, why wouldn't it be? I learned most of what I knew from him. We used to talk about the game all the time. I watched how he handled Sharman, how he handled Ramsey, how he handled Loscy and me, and the way he maneuvered his way through a minefield with the Cousy-Russell thing. I think one of the reasons he first thought of me as a coach was that he knew I was watching back then, and that I not only was aware of what he was doing but I understood why he was doing it.

He also knew I wasn't going to have a clash of egos with him. This is where he and Bill Fitch had trouble years later. If you're going to be coach of the Boston Celtics, the first thing you've got to realize is that it is Red Auerbach's team. He may not make you feel that way personally, but the press and the public do, because everything that happens in Boston is seen in the light of history. You never win a championship there; you win the *twelfth* championship, or the *fourteenth,* or the *sixteenth*. Celtic championships are like Super Bowls now; they all come with numbers.

Red's history was no problem for Russell, no problem for me, and it's no problem for KC Jones today, because it's *our* history, too; those flags up there belong to all of us.

Fitch was the exception. He hadn't been a part of *La Cosa Nostra*, so it's not difficult to understand how he felt. He had always been led to believe that winning an NBA championship was the ultimate goal, the ultimate accomplishment; and then when his team finally did it, the reaction of the fans was almost "So what?"—as if that's what they had been expecting him to do all along. It was, after all, the fourteenth championship. That meant Fitch wasn't getting a lot of the credit he deserved, and he deserved plenty. He was the guy who made the deal that brought Robert Parish and Kevin McHale to Boston for Joe Barry

Carroll. But everyone thought "Hey, Red did it again!" Fitch had a lot of trouble with that. It bothered him so much that it led him to a fight with Red for top billing, a fight he lost.

I wasn't going to have that kind of a problem.

The management training I had received in the insurance business was excellent preparation for coaching, even better than coaching a high school or college team, because coaching is pure management. I learned how to recruit, train, motivate, and manage people— all the skills you need to run a team. Most of the things they taught were things Red had been doing for years, things he just innately knew, I guess.

I based my management on the belief that there are two ways to motivate people: money and love.

Money was a motivating factor when I played. Contracts were not guaranteed back then, so you were really at the mercy of your coach. He had the authority to hire you and to fire you. That was a big stick to carry. Red always made it clear to us that our only security was in his pleasure with the way we performed our jobs; as long as he saw us playing hard, we'd have a home with the Celtics.

Then free agency came along, bringing with it long-term contracts for big money. It made sense for teams to peg their costs and plan their futures by locking up the services of their premier players; that's why Magic Johnson signed a twenty-five-year deal. He's not going anywhere, unless the Lakers want to send him somewhere, which is not too likely. So he knows he's got a job there for the rest of his career, yet because he's the kind of player he is, they don't have to worry about him dogging it.

That's not true of all secure players.

Darryl Dawkins is the perfect example. This guy could have been a monster, should have been a monster, but nobody had the controls. Armed with a long-term contract, Darryl had the security of dollars coming in. I've seen this happen so many times. Guys play hard to get that big contract, but then once they get it, say for five years, the next time they really put their asses into it is the last year of the deal, when they're looking for the next contract. In that long interim, however, all you're getting are half-assed efforts. It's not just the length of the contract that hurts, it's the length of the guaranteed life-style. Unless you're talking about athletes who are truly dedicated to the game, the only time these guys bear down is when their security is threatened.

I used to talk about this with Cousy, who began coaching the Kings in Cincinnati the same year I took the job in Boston. One night he started telling me about Sam Lacey, his rookie center—how he was pessimistic about him because Sam wouldn't do this, wouldn't do that, and just didn't take very well to coaching. "Cooz," I said, "I don't know what you expected. You guys just signed Sam for some very serious dough, didn't you? So obviously he must assume management thinks quite highly of him. And his wife certainly thinks he's great. His mother thinks he's great. His agent thinks he's great. You're the only guy telling him he's *not* great. So, Cooz, who do you think he's going to listen to?"

The days of motivating through money were gone. Now you had to motivate almost exclusively through love, as I was about to find out with Jo Jo White, a rookie guard whom we envisioned as a future leader of the Celtics.

Jo Jo was a tremendously proud guy, more temperamental than Sam Lacey ever thought of being and not at all willing to accept publicly the fact there were certain things about the game he did not know, particularly when it came to the fast break. He had played at Kansas, where the fast break did not exist. They danced to nothing but waltz music there, and here we were, getting ready to put on a rock show.

So at first I tried confronting him in front of the other players, trying to make it a challenge for him, but it quickly became obvious this was *not* the way to motivate Jo Jo White into becoming a better ballplayer. I couldn't yell at him the way Red yelled at me, so I took a page out of Red's book, remembering how he dealt with Russell, and I became Jo Jo's John the Baptist. It created problems with some of the other players who thought I was catering to him, though I tried dealing one-on-one with all of them at various times. If we were going to be a running team, I had to light a fire under Jo Jo. It was that simple.

He had to learn this thing called a fast break, but I didn't want to turn him off by telling him all that it encompassed and all that would be expected of him. I wanted to turn him *on.* So I made myself imagine he and I were about to climb the Matterhorn together. When you want someone who doesn't enjoy climbing to climb the Matterhorn with you, you don't bring him there on a bright sunny day, because he'll probably look up and say, "Hey, I can't climb that goddamn thing! I've never climbed a mountain in my life." No. You wait for a foggy day and then start walking up with him. Pretty soon you're in the clouds, so he never sees the top and never knows how far he still has to go. Once you get past that first layer of clouds, then you can say, "Jo Jo, look! You have only this much further to go before you can say you climbed the Matterhorn!"

It took time, but Jo Jo eventually reached the top.

I had a theory about the fast break. I used to tell it to my players all the time. *Anybody can be a bit of the Cooz!*

Cousy, once he gained possession of the ball, no longer felt compelled to know just where his teammates were. He knew from experience that they'd be running certain lanes on their ways to certain spots, and he knew when they'd get there. So what he did was read the defenses: *How many defenders are back there? What's my numerical advantage going to be?*

He would look at the defenders and add them up in his mind like a computer: *We've got three guys breaking in now. I'm going to see where our fourth guy is.* So he'd look for that fourth man, and if that fourth man had a step advantage on his defender, Cousy would arrange the attack to create an opening for him.

What I tried to teach my players was to read defenses the way Cousy did and react to those situations. Most coaches feel they have only one man to run their fast break, like a Magic Johnson, as if he's the only one capable of making it work. I never believed that was true. Anyone can run a fast break, as long as he doesn't start making passes he's incapable of completing. Big people don't have to make sensational passes; all they have to do is go one option beyond what the defense expects and they'll usually find a wide-open lane for that pass.

Cousy had inimitable skills. You can't ask anyone to do some of the things he did. But he also played with great intelligence, and that's what I did ask my players to do. *I asked them to think out there!*

And I wanted my players to be independent thinkers.

A "good" shot to me was this: *any* shot they thought they could make. But they had to be aware that if they missed that shot, someone else had to be in position to contend for the rebound. You always had to relate what you were doing to what your teammates were doing. In that respect, yes, guidelines were laid down. But I never wanted to be one of those coaches who legislate everything to their players: "Take no jump shots! All you take are layups! And never take a shot from more than fifteen feet!" That's paralyzing. There's no decision-making involved. Your players become robots.

I never wanted to coach robots. I wanted each of my guys to be independent, yet all of them to be unified. It began every year with fundamentals. Red was absolutely right about that. We worked on fundamentals for two solid weeks every fall. Then I turned them loose. I told them to watch for everything, interpret what they saw, and then react accordingly. *Make decisions*—that's what I wanted each of them to do; unless, of course, someone's decisions were wrong all the time. If that happened, I stepped in.

It didn't happen often.

One of those conflicts came with Don Chaney, who was Jo Jo's partner in the backcourt. He was a rookie the year before I started to coach, and he was the world's worst shooter. The worst! If he had been a baseball player he would have been Hoyt Wilhelm throwing the knuckler; that's how his shot used to look. It had a *side* rotation; it used to spin sideways, rather than with a normal rotation toward the basket.

He did all kinds of things wrong, but he was a super kid, very well-motivated, and he wanted to learn how to shoot. I wanted him to learn, too, because if he couldn't shoot, defenses would just sag away from him and start doubling up on somebody else. So I spent a lot of time working with him and he eventually got to a point where he became pretty effective.

He went through a stretch of games where he was scoring in the 20s. Now, all of a sudden, he was looking for the shot! He was looking for it so much that the ball wasn't getting into Havlicek's hands. He was out of his role, which was to be a rebounder and a good defensive player, to pass the ball, to advance it on the break, and to take the shot when it was there—*not* to look for it or go out of his way to create it. Our plays were designed to put the ball into the hands of our best shooters. That was Havlicek's role. Chaney, a great rebounder for a guard, was supposed to position himself by the boards. He'd have plenty of opportunities to score there, though they wouldn't get him the recognition that comes from hitting the outside shot all the time. What that positioning would do, however, was give us—a very small team—an extra rebounder.

So now Chaney got the flu. He was flat on his back for four or five days, then he comes back just as we are getting ready for a game down in Houston, his hometown, where all of his family is planning to attend. He's not at all grooved, because he's been sick, but he insists he's ready to play, so I put him out there and he's pathetic. Nothing goes right, and I can see he's really down.

The next game the same thing happens: He stinks out the joint. That's when I had to step in.

"Duck," I said, "is something bothering you? You know, I couldn't ask for a better player, and I've been delighted by your success. But these last two games, they haven't been Don Chaney games. What do you think we can do about it?"

He said, "I don't know." Then he started to think and zeroed in on his shooting.

"Look," I told him, "the reason you've been a great player for us, the reason we've been winning a lot of games with you, is that you give us something no one else can give us. But right now you're trying to give us things other people *can* give us. There's no other guard on this team who can rebound like you. No other guard can go in there for layups like you do, can fill the lane on fast breaks like you do, or has as much stamina as you have. We don't need 25 points from you. You scoring 25 points is not going to help us win. What is going to help us win are all of these other things you can do, things no one else can give us."

It was a classic example of the meaning of roles and of what can happen when someone steps out of his role and into someone else's.

He looked at me and said, "You're right," and went back to playing Don Chaney basketball. Other guys might have resisted and said: "What are you trying to do to me? After all this work, you're taking the ball out of my hands." Chaney didn't. He understood.

It helps to have the right kind of people.

I had a similar encounter with Paul Silas when he joined us at the start of my fourth season. He'd come to us from Phoenix, where he was the captain and an All-Pro, and now I was asking him to become our Sixth Man, the role Frank Ramsey made famous.

He was perfect for it. If you have a guy who's a specialist, who offers you some inordinate skill—Silas was a bear under the boards—you're much better off keeping him on the bench and starting the game with four top guys and a lesser player. This gives you an impact player to send in at the first substitution, someone who can pick up the pace of the game, increasing your efficiency with this special skill. The guy who shouldn't have started winds up giving you more productive minutes because he's playing with your best players, and now you are, in effect, bringing a legitimate starter off the bench just as the opposition is letting down.

If you've got that kind of player, like a Ramsey or a Havlicek, it makes all kinds of sense.

Silas was that kind of player. But when I suggested it to him he was not at all happy about it, nor was he very gracious. I tried explaining the theory of it to him and suggested that the role had become so celebrated in Boston that there was now more ego gratification in being our Sixth Man than there was in being just one out of five who started the game.

He finally gave in, but not happily, and he ended up on the cover of *Sports Illustrated*.

"I hated you," he told me later. "I thought you didn't understand the game, and that all this stuff about a 'special job' was just bullshit to cover your ass. But you were right. I've gotten more attention being the Sixth Man here than I ever got being an All-Pro out in Phoenix. I guess I was too immersed in my own egocentricity. Sorry."

But the pièce de résistance of my coaching from a technical standpoint, I thought, was making a champion center out of Dave Cowens. We revolutionized the position.

Cowens, to me, was Huckleberry Finn, a man of many causes. He became enthusiastic about so many things that the real challenge of coaching him was to keep up his enthusiasm for basketball and not allow him to spend it on all of these other endeavors. Car mechanic! Criminal science! Christmas tree farms! He never measured his enthusiasm for anything; he just put 100 percent of himself into everything.

One night, after a game in Portland, Oregon, Johnny Most and I went out for a couple of pops, then we had a bite to eat and headed back to the hotel. About a block ahead of us we saw Cowens coming out of an alley. I looked at Johnny and he looked at me as if to say: *What the hell is Dave Cowens doing in an alley?* We figured there must be a bar or a restaurant down there, but Cowens was gone by the time we got there, so we walked into this alley and looked around. There were no doors. No windows. No little stream of water on the ground. Nothing! We never found out what he was doing in there. It was probably just the adventurer in him. He had to find out what was in that alley, like the guy who climbed the mountain. Why did he climb the mountain? Because it was there! Why did Dave Cowens go into that alley? You guessed it. Because it was there.

Everyone thought you had to have a big guy at center. Cowens was not big. He was 6'8", shorter than Magic Johnson and Larry Bird.

My plan was to shuffle everyone around, to make those big guys on the other teams play a different kind of game when they faced us. But in order for that to happen, Cowens, who could already shoot well, was going to have to acquire additional skills. He was going to have to become a playmaker, too, able to pass the ball like a guard or a forward, which he'd never done before. He was also going to have to be able to pick out the right option in order to get that good pass to the right guy so that we could end up scoring.

So I devised a little exercise we used at practice every day, sort of like an Arthur Murray instruction kit. I'd have Cowens holler out the options as he ran through the steps of each play, just so he'd recognize them. Then I'd set up imaginary situations, and we'd discuss what he should look for whenever one of them occurred in a game: "What do you look for when *this* guy breaks free? When do you make your pass? What do you look for when you make your pass? What's going to trigger you to make that pass? Is it when the guy turns his head and puts down his hands for a second?"

Maybe I went a little too far. I didn't think so at the time, because there was so much involved, so much he had to learn. There were five decisions he had to make every time he got the ball, and I wanted him to recognize each one of them right away. That's why I had him call out the options: "This is a one! This is a three!"

Now we were in Buffalo for a game and my phone rang at three o'clock in the morning. It was Cowens. "I've got to talk with you right away," he said.

Damn! I figured he had gotten himself into trouble; maybe he'd had a few drinks and belted somebody. Or maybe he'd just gotten word of some terrible problem back home.

"Come right over," I said, hopping out of bed. Then I splashed cold water onto my face and waited for his knock.

He came in, sat down, and I asked him what was wrong.

"What do you think—I'm some kind of dumb ballplayer?"

"David," I replied, slowly, wanting to make certain I was hearing him right. "What do you mean?"

123

"Oh, you keep going over and over the same stuff, every day."

I was wide awake now.

"Dave," I told him, "if I thought you were dumb I would never have even contemplated doing what we're doing now. You're about to change this entire league's concept of the center position. No one has ever done what you're about to do. And you haven't done it either. Not yet. Okay, I admit there's a lot of repetition and I'm sure it does get tiresome. But what I'm trying to teach you is some of the real hair-splitting stuff that'll make you a little bit like Bob Cousy and a whole lot different from anyone else who's ever played the pivot in the NBA.

"Okay? Now good night. Thanks for coming over."

In 1973 I was named Coach of the Year, which was nice.

But in 1974, with Jo Jo and Chaney in the backcourt, Cowens ripping up the league at center, and Silas coming off our bench as Sixth Man—along, of course, with the All-Pro leadership of Havlicek and the steadying influence of Don Nelson—we won the championship.

That was better than any award. Hey, that was like old times again.

° 15 °

Pros and Prussian Generals

Will we ever see another Red Auerbach? Not likely.

But in terms of sustained success and overall approach to the game, Pat Riley comes the closest to Red, though KC Jones is up there, too. KC, of course, came directly out of the Celtics Tradition, whereas Pat inherited much of that same philosophy when he played for Bill Sharman.

Sharman, with KC as his assistant, coached the 1971–72 Lakers to a 69–13 record, including 33 wins in a row and an eventual championship. Riley was on that team, and it's my guess that he gained a lot of his insight into the handling of players by observing the way Sharman dealt with Wilt Chamberlain —the best job anyone ever did with him. Wilt was given input into everything that went on, and he enjoyed it so much, I was told, that he actually began to like practices, even though he was then thirty-five and in his thirteenth season. Over a fourteen-year career Wilt averaged 30.1 points a game, with a high-water average of 50.4 in 1961–62, yet in that championship season under Sharman he averaged only 14.8

while playing in all eighty-two games. He had traded in the big numbers for the big ring, and he was never happier. Wilt finally understood what *team* meant.

A great basketball team is like a jazz group having a jam session at three o'clock in the morning in some smoky joint. The best jazz groups are the ones that know when to let a guy do his solo, how to back him up, how to make him look good, how to complement him so that they all can make beautiful music together. There's a lot of ego involved, but there's a lot of teamwork, too, because if this guy keeps doing his solo and never allows anybody else to come in, the boys in the band are going to get a little bit upset: "Hey, I want to do *my* number, too!"

The people who've been in the business a long time understand that, so they don't continually write all the music. They don't just hand out sheets to everyone and say, "Play my music," because they understand they've got all these great improvisational people here, people who are going to become very frustrated if they're made to play somebody else's music all the time, or if every time they attempt to add an extra note they hear the conductor tapping his little stick as if to say: "What's going on over there? I want you to stop it at once."

A players' coach understands this, too, and Pat and KC are perfect examples of what's meant by a players' coach; both allow great player input. This is how you get a real commitment from your players.

The best illustration of commitment I've seen in the current era was in the final round of the 1987 playoffs, when the Celtics took the Lakers to six games before LA eliminated them, despite the fact that Kevin McHale and Bill Walton played with broken bones in their feet, Robert Parish played with a recurring ankle sprain, and Danny Ainge played with a sprained knee.

When people want to knock KC Jones as a coach, they first ought to look at that series. In this day and age, with all the money that's involved and with players ever on the alert for career-ending injuries, making them more prone to protecting their futures than they are to pushing themselves through any kind of pain, the way those Celtics continued to put out for KC was nothing less than a tribute to good coaching. And I've seen the Lakers do the same thing for Pat.

Riley, I think, is a genius at taking talent and figuring out the optimum way to use it. He's also the leading exponent of fast-break basketball in the NBA today. He's elevated the fast break into *offensive pressure* basketball that's miles ahead of what other people, some with very good talent at their disposal, are trying to do. His teams are doing what the teams I played on did, constantly applying pressure to the defense, never walking with the ball—he's polished that aspect of the game to the *n*th degree.

Riley's Lakers put opposing defenses through a physical torture test every night, rushing the ball at them, forcing them into mistakes, making them get tired. And they execute beautifully. Again, I see the influence of Sharman, who's now the Lakers' president, although Pat was also exposed to the fast break at Kentucky where he played for Adolph Rupp, a coach who understood tempo basketball. But that Sharman team on which Riley played was almost a replica of the Cousy-Russell Celtics: Chamberlain, the outlet man, would rebound the ball and then kick it out to Jerry West or Gail Goodrich, who'd push it up, with speed merchants like Happy Hairston and Jim McMillian cruising the forward lanes. They killed teams with that fast break.

So Riley, reflecting all he's observed and experienced, is the consummate attack coach today, fast becoming a master at it, which is what makes him the closest thing to Red Auerbach I've ever seen.

And KC Jones? As tough a guy as you'd ever want to have on your side, and just as loyal. KC is a balls-to-the-wall guy who overcame a drinking problem, then overcame a crushing disappointment when the Bullets fired him in 1976 after he brought them a three-year record of 155–91. They thought he wasn't strong enough. Why? Because he had allowed his assistant, Bernie Bickerstaff, to address the team during a timeout, and when the TV cameras picked it up, people misinterpreted KC's lack of ego as a sign of weakness. That bum rap not only followed him for years; it damn near ended his career.

But Pat and KC aren't the only coaches I admire. I think Doug Moe is one of the few coaches in the NBA today who totally understands what the pro game is all about. He's never had a lot of talented people to work with, yet he's always had a competitive team. His clubs keep the heat on you all night long. You don't want to spend too much time studying the rosters when you play a Doug Moe team, because his teams don't look too good on paper. What you want to do when you're getting ready to face a Doug Moe team is tell yourself, "If we aren't careful, these guys are gonna whip our butts tonight." One thing is certain: They'll be in your face all night. Doug understands what freedom of expression and freedom of interpretation mean to a player, plus he's not afraid to use every man on his bench.

He's very definitely a players' coach.

So was Billy Cunningham when he was with the 76ers. Billy was a tough cookie; he did a super job there. Al Attles: another coach I had great respect for, another players' coach. Gene Shue's that way; so is Lennie Wilkens.

All of these guys had something in common, something that made them uniquely qualified to become players' coaches, to earn the respect and receive the commitment they all got from those players.

That common thread was that they had all been players, too.

When expansion came along, it brought with it a great infusion of college coaches into the NBA. I call them Prussian generals: "You *vill* go to dat spot dere, and you *von't* move from dere!" They don't want their players to think; everything is pre-thought-out for them by the coach.

That was pure Hubie Brown. That's why he had trouble with Patrick Ewing. He wanted to make him into a forward, a position with which the kid was totally unfamiliar.

If you're going to do something like that, and you're a smart coach, you first want to sell the player on the concept, particularly if he happens to be one of your better players. You want to make him see how this will help him, how it will increase his effectiveness, how it will be beneficial to his whole game. You want to make him believe that he'll become an even better player if he does what you're asking him to do. So you bring him along on your train of thought. That's what Auerbach did all the time. But Hubie couldn't do that because Hubie had to be *the boss*. So it was: "Patrick, you are now a forward." Simple as that.

It's always "my system" with these Prussian generals.

A few years ago, when I was watching the Knicks play the Pistons at Detroit in preparation for a CBS telecast, Bernard King went absolutley crazy—he had a *wonderful* game! Hubie spent the night running around screaming numbers—"Twenty-two! Seventeen! Nineteen!"—whatever he screamed, it seemed Bernard always wound up with the ball and scored. One of the CBS people sitting next to me asked, "Tommy, what do those numbers Hubie keeps shouting mean?" I said, "That's how many seconds the other guys get to hold the ball before they decide they'd better give it to Bernard." When the game ended we went into the Knicks' locker room, where Hubie was ecstatic, talking with the writers. But was he telling them Bernard had a wonderful game? No. He was telling them, "What pleased me most was that Bernard scored all of his points *within the system.*"

Give me a break.

When things went wrong, of course, it was never the fault of the system. College coaches are great at covering their own asses; they're great shifters of blame. They remind me of a Benny Hill line: "He who laughs when things go wrong has found someone to blame them on!"

That's what they do all the time. They're trained in the political arts, and their players understand this. Patrick Ewing is no dummy. He knew if Hubie's plan didn't work, there was no way in the world it was going to be Hubie's fault. It was going to be Patrick's fault, because Patrick didn't execute Hubie's plan well enough.

That's one of the big differences between the college coach and the ex-player coach. Did you ever hear Pat Riley place the blame on one of his players in public? Or KC Jones? Or Gene Shue? Or Billy Cunningham? Or Don Nelson? No, because they were players, too, and they understand it doesn't do a damn bit of good. It's just a protective device for an insecure coach, a coach who quickly becomes the enemy in the eyes of his players.

The way the Prussian generals see it, the coach's ego is to be protected at all costs, even if it means making scapegoats out of his players. It's easy to do that in college, to get the message across in the media that you really don't have all the "material" you need, even though the coach who's whispering this to the writers is the same coach who recruited the "material."

There are *beaucoup* colleges trying to become the NCAA champion, but there's only one winner, so these guys have come up with another ploy lately: Now you're great if you make it to the Final Four! That's the new criterion for greatness. It's a joke. But they believe it. Hubie Brown coached for ten years in the NBA and his biggest accomplishment was taking the Celtics to seven games in the 1984 playoffs. He made that sound as if he'd won the damn championship! But if you ask a Pat Riley, a Don Nelson, or a Billy Cunningham what it means to take the Celtics to seven, they'll tell you flat-out:"Baby, it means you lost!"

The biggest challenge for a guy like Hubie would be to coach players who are really talented, and he had considerable talent on his teams in New York, he just failed to get the best out of it. He was always at his best with players of lesser talent, where fear could be used to control them, because, like most college coaches, he was afraid to give up control, to allow his players to become involved.

That's all part of their philosophy of survival. It's coaching out of fear, or out of ridicule. It's naming names if you have to, anything to divert responsibility for the failures of the "system." But the coach who creates fear in his players will never get the best out of them, and I'll guarantee you something else: Any coach who serves up his players as scapegoats will be there only until those players are no longer afraid of him. The moment they sense he's in trouble, they'll die on him. That's just human nature.

Hubie did it by pointing fingers.

Bill Fitch does it with biting humor. His wit is so sharp that, in every encounter, he tries to put his players on the defensive in a humorous way. He thinks it's funny, but a joke doesn't work unless the other guy laughs, and more than a few of Bill's players have resented his attempts to make them the butt of his gags and one-liners.

Bobby Knight, in many ways, is the classic college

coach. If I were to sketch a cartoon of Bobby I'd show him with the reddest face possible, up in the air, waving his fists with his feet askew, after a water bucket has just been kicked.

He makes his players very competitive, he makes them masters of certain techniques, but he's very tough about it. I don't know how much depth there is to his relationship with his players; I suspect there's probably more than I think there is, but I would never have wanted to play for Bobby Knight. I could never play for a guy who, when I thought I was giving my best out there, would scream at me when I came back to the bench. I'm the one who's supposed to have his emotions raised and he's the one who's supposed to be directing those emotions, yet he's the one who's out of control!

Red never hollered at players when they came out of a game. You'll never see Pat Riley or KC Jones do it, either.

I guess Bobby thinks it's effective. Maybe it is. But you'd have to be an awfully unusual kid to withstand that kind of abuse and still play your heart out for the guy.

Most kids would resent that, I think.

I know most pros sure do.

But it's more than just knowing how to handle his personnel that makes a college coach effective at the pro level. In many ways, the pro game is an altogether different game.

After being accustomed to having four weeks, maybe even six weeks, of two-a-day practices—I've even heard of three-a-days!—to set up his agenda for the year, the college coach coming into the NBA now finds he has just ten days of two-a-days and then any practices he can squeeze in once the season gets under way to put in his entire system, offense and defense.

That alone should be reason enough to change from

a "my way" approach to a willingness to relinquish some interpretation, some freedom of expression, to his players.

Then there are the rigors of an eighty-two-game season. How do you keep guys motivated that long, especially if you're faced with a rebuilding year? And what's this stuff about a twenty-four-second clock?

And then what about the playoffs? They truly are the second season, as everyone calls them. How do you win a four-out-of-seven series? That's something these coaches never had to deal with in college. In college you win by 30, then lose by 30 the next night to the same team. Now what? Do you change your whole system? Or do you simply make adjustments? If so, *what* adjustments? Do you practice more? Or are you practicing too much, adding to your players' fatigue?

This is completely outside of the college coach's understanding. Maybe he's seen it or heard about it or talked about it, but he's never experienced it. Life is a lot less complicated in the NCAA: It's won and done, or see you later.

So it takes time to learn how to coach in the NBA.

Another thing the newly arrived college coach has difficulty doing is properly utilizing his bench. He's just not used to employing those seventh, eighth, and ninth players effectively, but they have to be used in the pros, especially if you're up against a team that likes to play tempo basketball.

When I was coaching we used to include poor substitutions by these college guys as part of our game plans. Dick Motta was one we exploited all the time because he wouldn't take out players when they obviously needed a rest. Jack Ramsay, even after he'd been in the league for a while, was another one who hated to go to his bench, who had some kind of aversion to using that one extra player. So these guys were tailor-made for us. We were the smallest team in the league. All we had going for us was speed and quickness, but we knew if we kept applying that pressure we could always count on their clubs to fall apart from weariness at some point down the stretch run.

The first year I coached, the season between Russell's retirement and the arrival of Cowens, I had three centers: Hank Finkel, Richie Johnson, and Bad News Barnes, probably none of whose careers are recalled today by anyone other than family and close friends. It was also the year the Knickerbockers won the first of their two championships. We went 34–48 that year and didn't even make the playoffs—yet we were 4–3 against the Knicks! Why? Because Red Holzman would not take Willis Reed out of the game.

Even an old pro like Red got caught in that trap.

Willis, who did not like to run, was far more talented physically than any one of my three centers; he could have beaten up on any one of them. But I platooned them, so that all three kept coming at him, one at a time, forcing him to chase them, and by the time the fourth quarter arrived, poor Willis—who was 60, maybe 70 percent of the New York offense—would have trouble keeping his legs underneath him. We never allowed him to walk. We just sapped his strength. It was like cutting off Samson's hair.

That's why good substitutions are an essential coaching skill.

Yet for all of their weaknesses, for all of their lack of understanding about the pro game, these Prussian generals would look at the ex-player coaches as if we were an affront to them, as if we weren't entitled to be on the same court with them, as if they somehow knew all the basketball there was to know.

What's more, they were cliquey, like baseball managers. It's their political instinct to band together. You rarely see ex-player coaches that friendly before a game, because the competitiveness is still there.

Those old tribal rivalries are quickly rekindled. But the Prussian generals have no such inhibitions. They're still buddy-buddy.

I was president of the Coaches Association when Hubie Brown attended his first meeting in 1976, and before it was half over he was trying to change the rules.

But that's not why I don't like him. I'll tell you why I don't like him.

I love and respect Larry Costello; on Larry's worst day, he was three times the coach Hubie ever thought of being. Hubie was a high school coach who hooked on as an assistant to Vic Bubas at Duke. Then, when Bubas and his staff were let go, Hubie called Larry, who was coaching at Milwaukee, asking him for help.

Larry made him his assistant. He saved his ass! Within two years Hubie was carving him up. That's why I don't like Hubie Brown.

Part of Hubie's infrequent success was a gimmick other teams weren't prepared for, but I disliked him so much that whenever we were scheduled to play him, even if we'd already played three games in a row on the road, I'd have a special practice just to get my guys ready. Then we'd kick his ass, and afterward I'd tell reporters that what his gimmick really consisted of was a lousy high school zone defense.

He'd get furious. Too bad. It was true.

Hubie, who was a loser at Atlanta before he became an even bigger loser in New York, was nevertheless an elitist who thought ex-players knew nothing, that in order to be a truly outstanding coach you had to have paid your dues at the high-school level. He actually put that in writing in a 1983 *Sports Illustrated* piece that was modestly entitled "The Gospel According to Hubie."

It read, in part: "Down at one level you've got

some children who were players—guys like Billy Cunningham and Kevin Loughery—who never coached a game and walked into jobs where there was all kinds of talent. Then you've got all the other guys, who I personally have no problem with. And way up here—so far from the rest of them we're practically on an island—you've got Jack Ramsay, Dick Motta and me."

He's a beauty.

Now let's look at the thirteen coaches who have won the championships since 1970, the first year after the Russell dynasty ended.

Nine of them were ex-players.

And let's see how long it took them all to do it.

Among the ex-players, Pat Riley (Los Angeles, 1982) won in his first year; Larry Costello (Milwaukee, 1971) and Bill Sharman (Los Angeles, 1972) won in their third years; KC Jones (Boston, 1984) won in his fourth year; I (Boston, 1974) won in my fifth year; Al Attles (Golden State, 1975) and Billy Cunningham (Philadelphia, 1983) won in their sixth years; and Red Holzman (New York, 1970) and Lenny Wilkens (Seattle, 1979) won in their seventh years.

Among the four college coaches who've won in that time, Paul Westhead (Los Angeles, 1980) was an aberration. Replacing Jack McKinney, who was injured in a freak bicycle accident, Westhead won in his first attempt, then was fired at the start of his third season. Jack Ramsay (Portland, 1977) was in his ninth year before he won his first title; Dick Motta (Washington, 1978) was in his tenth year; and Bill Fitch (Boston, 1981) was in his eleventh year.

The fact is, contrary to Hubie's gospel, most of the ex-players did it within five years while the college coaches needed an average of ten.

One of the biggest challenges facing the NBA, especially now that it's in the throes of expansion again, is to find those coaches who will bring out the best in the game.

Where is it going to find them? The hope here is that it will take a closer look at those players who've distinguished themselves throughout their careers, that it will keep an eye out for the Rileys, Joneses, Sharmans, and Cunninghams of tomorrow.

They're out there somewhere, and they're the answer.

They're the ones best-equipped to pass the torch of NBA excitement to the next generation.

The Prussian generals? They can go back to getting their jollies from making it all the way into the Final Four.

◦ **16** ◦

It All Starts at the Top

A little bit of knowledge is not the most dangerous thing in sports, although it's dangerous enough. The most dangerous thing in sports is to know a little and think you know a lot.

Nowhere is this more apparent than in ownerships.

Strength always starts at the top—institutions are reflections of the people who run them—and nothing can ruin a good franchise any faster than a bad ownership.

The teams that survive are the teams that remain relatively stable at the top, that are run by good basketball people who know what they're looking for in players and in coaches.

Look at the Knicks, perhaps the most financially stable of all franchises. They've never had stability at the top or a consistent philosophy on how to win, how to build a ballclub, how to suffer defeat and bounce back from it.

Eddie Donovan was the second most-informed person in the history of the NBA when it came to building teams. He was right behind Auerbach in that

department. He was one who built the great Knickerbockers team that won championships in 1970 and
1973.

Then Gulf + Western took control of the franchise
and hired Sonny Werblin, who in one of the dumbest
bureaucratic power plays of all time maneuvered Eddie into a little office downstairs by the boiler room.

He wasn't next to the furnace; he was *under* it.

Eddie was a basketball man. He was not a politician, not politically oriented enough to deal with all
that was going on in Madison Square Garden at the
time. He didn't know how to play those games within
the corporate structure, nor did he care to play them,
so they aced him right out of the organization.

He left and went to Buffalo for five years, where he
turned an expansion team into a playoff contender.
Those Braves of his were one of the toughest teams I
ever coached against.

What fascinated me, watching all of this from Boston, was how no one in the New York organization
was willing to link Eddie's departure to the Knicks'
subsequent fall from power. It was made to seem like
a coincidence, but there was nothing coincidental about
it at all. Eddie was a man who had a history of
winning wherever he went. Two years after that team
he built won its second title, the Knickerbockers had
a losing record again, the first of three in a row.

That's what a *little* knowledge can do for you.

Sonny Werblin, running the show for Gulf + Western, finally realized what they had lost and wisely
brought Eddie back as general manager, giving him
instructions to put their Humpty Dumpty together.
By 1980–81 Eddie had the Knicks looking good,
50–32.

That's when Werblin got involved again.

He kicked Donovan upstairs into a VP slot and
brought in Dave DeBusschere, making him director
of basketball operations—in effect, general manager,
Eddie's old job.

Then he cut both of their parachutes.

Somehow Hubie Brown, who's got a great knack for making himself sound like Albert Einstein, managed to impress the hell out of Sonny, enough so that Werblin gave him the coaching job.

Now Sonny had a coach whose philosophies were diametrically opposed to those held by his general manager, which meant that his Knicks, like a house divided against itself, were destined for disaster once more.

I can remember working New York games on television and going into the john at the half, listening to DeBusschere and Donovan saying to each other, "Boy, if only we could run!"

Like most longtime NBA people, they understood that the way to win in this league is to run. There's no other way to be a consistent winner. Yet here they were, saddled with a coach who didn't believe that.

Hubie fought them all the way. This was Hubie's team, and things were going to be done Hubie's way, and nothing was going to change that . . . until Hubie tried to screw around with Patrick Ewing's head, and Patrick stopped functioning.

The Knicks had paid an awful lot of money for Ewing, expecting him to be great, and when it became obvious he wasn't going to achieve anything close to greatness under Hubie, Scotty Stirling, who had replaced DeBusschere as GM, stepped in and Hubie was gone.

It was a very expensive lesson.

Yet it remains a lesson that a surprising number of seemingly intelligent people have still failed to comprehend.

I have the utmost respect for the owner in Los Angeles, Jerry Buss, because he supports whatever his management team tells him is best for the ball club. He surrounds himself with sound basketball people— Bill Sharman, Jerry West, Pat Riley—then accedes to their suggestions.

I'm sure Buss has an ego and a half, yet you never see him popping off in public. You never see any big displays of self-aggrandizement to show that he's in charge. If anything, he's exhibited great patience; he doesn't seem to panic.

Yet I'm also sure he challenges his people to fight him for what they really believe in. Once he sees how strongly they feel, once he understands the meat of the matter, he usually goes along with them.

He's like the players' coach who permits his players to have substantial input.

That's what a good owner does; he allows his basketball people to run the basketball operation, and he does it by allowing them independence, even when it means independence from him.

Jerry Buss is my idea of a great owner.

Harold Katz, on the other hand, strikes me as the type of owner who's inclined to run roughshod over his coach, or over anybody who doesn't stand right up to him.

He was making inflammatory statements about Moses Malone long before he traded him for Jeff Ruland, which certainly leads to a suspicion that he was so hell-bent on getting rid of Malone that he wrecked his team in the process. Ruland played only five games for Philadelphia before his bad knee forced him into premature retirement at age twenty-seven.

Didn't the 76ers know the full extent of those medical possibilities?

Or did their owner's impulsiveness force them into a grave mistake? It would have been very easy for them to give Ruland only a cursory examination, because, thanks to Katz, a deal for Moses *had* to be made. They weren't going to get anything more out of the guy if he stayed.

Of course, it *is* the owner's team.

So I guess that means he's free to do whatever he wants with it, which includes making a mess of it.

When I was coaching, a very significant thing happened to the owners' support for the coaches.

They agreed that if there weren't enough first-class seats on a plane for all of the players to sit in that section, the coach would have to give up his seat and go to the back.

In my mind that was symbolic of the low regard these owners, many of whom were new to the game, had for the coaches. These were the same guys who brought in all those Prussian generals, so I suppose I shouldn't have been too surprised.

As president of the Coaches Association I was very upset by this rule. Many of the other coaches were upset, too, but because they feared their owners, they capitulated. I went right to Red. "Look," I said, "if I'm supposed to be the leader of this team, the number-one man in our traveling troupe, and I have some rookie bump me out of my seat as if I'm a second-class citizen, there is no way I am going to be able to maintain the respect of my players."

Red said he agreed with the point, but that these new owners were a different breed of cat. Nevertheless, he said, he'd see what could be done. Nothing was done, at least while I was still coaching.

Later, after I'd left the Celtics, I saw him one day and thought about it again.

"Red," I asked, "did you guys ever solve that problem about the coaches having to go to the back of the plane?"

"Tommy," he said, "they took care of it."

"Oh?" I asked. "How so?"

"If there aren't enough seats for the coach and his players in first class now," he explained, "then the coach waits and takes the next plane."

They missed the whole point.

Then again, maybe they didn't. Maybe they just didn't care.

Since 1964, when Walter Brown, their founder, died, the Celtics have gone through fourteen ownerships. These have run the gamut from openly adoring to unabashedly avaricious, but through them all Auerbach has been a steadying influence.

He certainly was my main source of strength when I took the coaching job. We had a major rebuilding project on our hands, and though it took us only three seasons to get back into the playoffs, there was plenty of grumbling from fans who had grown accustomed to not just making the playoffs every year, but to *winning* them every year. Yet while everyone else was looking at the scoreboard, Red was looking at the realities, and I never felt any undue pressure from him.

But the greatest thing he was able to do was turn all of those owners, with a couple of exceptions, into *Celtics* owners. He got them to adopt the principles of the way he ran the team: *Show patience. Don't panic. Allow the kids time to grow.*

Boston has always displayed that needed patience. So has Los Angeles. Now we're seeing it in Utah, too, where the owner, Larry Miller, has placed the destiny of his ball club in the hands of Frank Layden. It's taken time, but Layden has brought the Jazz from points A to B to C, to where they're now a very competitive team. Frank's another one of these college coaches who needed time to learn how to win in the NBA, but one of the things he knew right away was the importance of occasionally turning his players loose. His main problem now is that he's also the one who negotiaties their contracts, so while it may be true they have no beef with Happy Frank, their coach, there's still a good chance they're apt to get steamed at Slapsy-Maxie, the guy who holds the purse strings.

For me, Red's support was essential.

How can the armies hit the beaches on D-day if

they're not sure their generals are going to support them?

When you're not sure of your general's support, when you're not confident you've got his full backing, you don't stray far from your foxhole, baby. You're busy keeping yourself low to the ground so that you don't get picked off by a sniper's bullet. Instead of getting up and charging, knowing the general is guarding your back—"I'm moving full-speed ahead, sir! Don't let those bastards get me"—you begin looking over your shoulder; and, man, you ain't never gonna get to Berlin that way.

Red represented a supportive general to me.

That's what he represented to a lot of people in the organization.

Then an owner named Irv Levin came along, disrupting the entire franchise, second-guessing everyone, including Red.

It was like Harry Truman ordering Douglas MacArthur to pocket his pistol and come home from Korea in 1951.

The general was in trouble.

And if the general was in trouble, you can just imagine how the army felt.

Giving 'em the hook *(courtesy of Joe Fitzgerald)*.

Fighting for a Holy Cross rebound against Duquesne's Si Green, 1955 *(UPI/Bettman Newsphotos).*

The 1956–57 Celtics. *Front row, left to right:* Lou Tsioropoulos, Andy Phillip, Frank Ramsey, Red Auerbach, Bob Cousy, Bill Sharman, Jim Loscutoff. *Standing, left to right:* Walter A. Brown, Dick Hemric, Jack Nichols, Bill Russell, Arnie Risen, Tommy Heinsohn, Harvey Cohn, and Lou Pieri *(courtesy of the Boston Celtics).*

With Wilt Chamberlain in the 1962 Eastern Division playoffs *(AP/ Wide World Photos).*

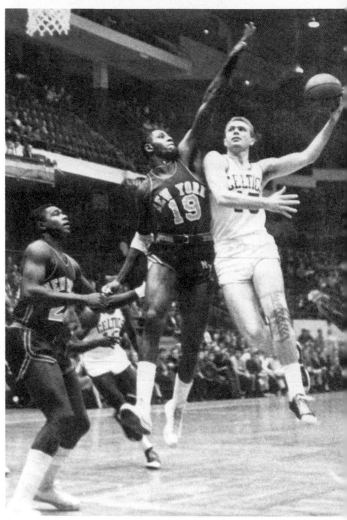

Guarded by Willis Reed, with Jim Barnes looking on, 1964 *(UPI/Bettman Newsphotos)*.

As coach
(*courtesy of the
Boston Celtics*).

Unhappy with referee Bob Rakel's call; General Manager Red Auerbach is on the right (*UPI/Bettman Newsphotos*).

The 1973–74 Celtics. *Front row, left to right:* Jo Jo White, Don Chaney, John Havlicek, Red Auerbach, Bob Schmertz, Tommy Heinsohn, Dave Cowens, Paul Silas, John Killilea. *Standing, left to right:* Mark Volk, Dr. Sam Kane, Paul Westphal, Phil Hankinson, Steve Downing, Don Nelson, Hank Finkel, Steve Kuberski, Art Williams, Dr. Tom Silva, Frank Challant *(courtesy of the Boston Celtics).*

At the victory party for the 1976 Celtics *(courtesy of the Boston Herald).*

**With Red
Auerbach, at
1985 game
honoring Red
*(UPI/Bettman
Newsphotos)*.**

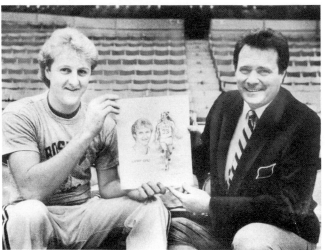

**With Larry Bird and Heinsohn's drawing of him
(courtesy of the Boston Herald).**

With John Havlicek *(left)* **and Bill Russell** *(courtesy of the* Boston Herald*).*

Next to his
plaque at the
Basketball
Hall of Fame
*(AP/Wide
World Photos).*

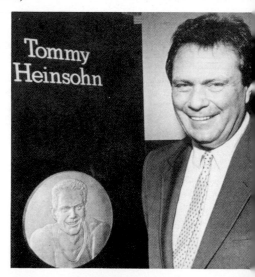

° 17 °

No Harm, No Foul

It may come as a surprise to some people to learn I have enormous respect for referees.

I'm sure it will come as a surprise to referees.

But it's true.

First of all, refereeing a basketball game is one of the most difficult jobs in all of sports. The referee is a judge. He embodies the laws of the game, laws that have been codified, and it's his responsibility to interpret them, then enforce them, all the while enduring tremendous public pressure because he's performing this task in front of fifteen thousand lobbyists.

That's what fans are: They're lobbyists, a pressure group trying their best to influence a referee's decision —"We want you to enforce the law this way!" And they're poised to give him an immediate "Yea!" or "Nay!" every time he blows his whistle.

A referee's decisions have to be made very quickly, and unlike other sports, where officials are allowed to take time to confer with their peers—"Was he safe? Was he out? What do you think? How did you see

145

it?''—the basketball referee is pretty much on his own.

The sheer quantity of decisions he's called upon to make amazes me. No human being is going to be right 100 percent of the time, and yet every one of those decisions can be vital to a game.

It takes only a handful of out-of-bounds plays going one way instead of the other to dramatically affect an outcome. An out-of-bounds play seems pretty innocuous. But if a team is awarded, say, six possessions it otherwise wouldn't have had, and that team shoots 50 percent, that means it's getting three more baskets than it otherwise would have gotten, and of course the other team is getting three fewer baskets than it might have gotten. So you're talking about a potential spread of 12 points, more than the average winning margin of most games, all resting on a decision as basic as: "Who touched the ball last?"

The referee's decisions also determine who will be permitted to remain in the game and how much emotion a team or player will be permitted to express. That's extremely important to some teams and players who pour great amounts of emotion into their games. The official who decides to put a damper on that emotion, perhaps by calling a close game, limiting physical contact, is seriously impairing the overall effectiveness of those teams and players, which is why all coaches have their own lists of referees they do and do not want to see. But those lists are often conditional. There are some refs you want on the road yet don't want at home, because you know they can't be intimidated by a crowd; the emotions of the event are not going to consume them.

All in all, it takes someone with an unusual personality to be a good referee, to continue doing his job well night after night in city after city when he knows every time he blows that whistle someone's going to tell him, "You stink!"

These guys must have a difficult time establishing an image with their kids. I don't know how they do it.

The second thing that amazes me about them is that they're constantly being put through a physical torture test while making these decisions, a torture test quite unlike those imposed by any other sport. They're being pushed to the brink of physical fatigue, even exhaustion, yet they're still expected to hand down these magnificent, grandiose pronouncements while their stamina's being sapped.

You can't ask a player to go all-out for 48 minutes every night without giving him a breather now and then, but there are no substitutions for referees, who are withstanding the same heat, pressure, and pace as the players, and doing it at a more advanced age.

I always admired them.

That is not, however, to say I always got along with them.

A coach will always plead for his own self-interest, and many of them regularly go beyond normal courtroom decorum in making those pleas. I was certainly one of them, especially if I thought a referee was subjective. Some of them get that way. They'll never admit it, but they decide at some point along the line that they don't like a certain coach.

Mendy Rudolph, for instance, never liked me. Or so I thought.

We really had it out once.

We were playing the Knicks in a key game at Madison Square Garden, and one of my players took a shot at the end of the first half, just as the buzzer was about to go off. As he did that, one of the Knicks jumped up and grabbed the net, which is an automatic goaltending call. The ball hadn't reached the rim yet, but if they touch the net the call is supposed to be automatic.

We didn't get the call, so as we were walking off the court I said, "C'mon, Mendy, that's an automatic!"

Mendy looked at me and said, "Heinsohn, will you stop grandstanding!"

That's what I mean by a referee having a subjective view of a coach that colors everything that coach tries to tell him.

Some coaches have tried to use that charge to intimidate referees. There are some referees who can be intimidated. Mendy, who died a few years ago, wasn't one of them.

The summer after that game I saw him at the league meetings in Phoenix and pulled him aside. "Mendy," I said, "I think we've got something to talk about. I've got a feeling you're subjective about the way I coach a game. . . ."

So we hashed the whole thing out. He walked away with a better understanding of where I was coming from, and I walked away with a better understanding of where he was coming from. I never thought he was being subjective again, and he never felt I was grandstanding. In fact we ended up doing a Miller Lite commerical together, the one where he wouldn't let me finish my beer. Remember?—"Heinsohn, you're outta the bar!"

Everybody wants to get the best end of the legal battle in court, to be awarded the multimillion-dollar settlement—on each decision, okay? So you plead your case any way you can. Now admittedly, I would never have been mistaken for Perry Mason, though there have been coaches who've played that role in various ways. One of my problems was that I'm a big guy. It's hard for big guys to be inconspicuous when they want to be. Sometimes I wanted to be. But I'd stand up and get a technical foul for standing up. Or I'd turn my back to the referee, not saying anything to him, and still get a technical because he thought I was saying something to the crowd to show him up. The bigger you are the more you're noticed, and if there's one thing referees don't want, it's coaches being noticed, because then they suspect you're making a comment on every call.

When Red Holzman coached the Knicks, he used far worse verbiage on the refs than I ever thought of, and I was no pansy. A lot of my stuff had to be deleted—but some of the things Red came out with hadn't been seen in print since the Middle Ages. But because he was a little guy who never got off the bench, he could say anything he wanted to, which made him very effective in his own way.

One night in Boston Garden, however, he got off the bench, walked onto the court, and proceeded to cuss out this ref. Now, I was watching with great interest, because when you walk onto the court it's supposed to be an automatic technical foul. Red was almost at halfcourt now, near the center jump circle, and I was sitting on our bench, waiting for the call. But still no foul was called. So now I got up just to put my own heat on the ref, to let him know I was watching what Red was doing. Red saw me coming and said, "Tommy, these guys have no balls." Nothing happened. Even Red looked a little surprised at that. So now he said it louder: "Tommy, these guys have no *fuckin'* balls!" I looked at the refs. No whistle! I turned to Holzman and said, "Red, pal, I guess you're right." Then I shook my head and walked back to our bench as he walked back to his.

I admired Red. He rarely got off the bench, so maybe that gave him the benefit of the doubt and created the appearance that his beef was legitimate.

I was different. I was very animated. I was conducting my own lobbying exercises every night, not only to keep the refs on their toes, but also to keep my own team charged up because we were the smallest team in the league. I wanted my guys emotionally charged because speed was the name of our game. If I sat on the bench sucking my thumb—which wasn't my nature anyway—I wouldn't be conveying any emotion. Plus I wanted to be emotionally involved, too, so sometimes I'd step out of line for effect, and sometimes I'd actually get mad.

What a coach really hopes to do, however he does it, is to influence the trend of the calls, rather than any individual call itself. John Havlicek relied on quickness, speed, and continuous movement, so if another player was allowed to maintain physical contact with John, with no fouls being called, that had a very definite influence on our game. Yet if the referee had it in the back of his mind that he didn't want to see a Bill Bradley forced out of the game on six hand-checking fouls, he'd call one, just to establish that Bradley couldn't have his hands all over Havlicek all night. He then might call a second one to reinforce the message: "Hey, loosen up on Havlicek." My objective would be to have him make those calls early. Those calls were very meaningful to us.

But there's no consistency from referee to referee on calls like hand-checking or three-second violations. That's why it's important to get a trend established early, a trend that will be favorable to your team. That's what a good coach does. If a Wilt Chamberlain or a Kareem Abdul-Jabbar was allowed to spend more than three seconds in the lane, that obviously increased his chances of scoring against us, so I was always up yelling, "Three seconds! Three seconds!" Hey, four seconds might have killed us.

Some referees had a sense of humor. You could kid with them.

Sid Borgia was the dean of officials when I played. They gave Sid the rule book on a Friday and by Sunday he knew more than the book did. He had his own way of defining a foul, which basically went like this: *No harm, no foul*. If someone didn't bleed, Sid didn't call a foul. He would allow great contact, then every once in a while he'd become very strict, but at least there was a sameness to his calls at both ends of the court.

Sometimes Sid made up his rules as he went along. One night I drove hard to the basket against Syracuse, smashing right into Bobby Hopkins. We collided in midair and both landed on the floor. A whistle blew. We were both tangled up on the floor when Sid walked over, looked down, and told Bobby: "No walk, no foul, no nothing. You shoot two." They're still trying to figure out how to enter that one into the scorebook.

Every year I'd try to think of a new way to lobby Sid for free throws without having to spill blood first. One year I tried yelling at him to get him mad. It didn't work. He just kicked me out of the game. He loved doing that. So then I tried total disdain. Every time he'd call a foul on me I'd just stand there, staring him up and down, not saying a word, but with a look that clearly said: "You idiot." It didn't bother Sid a bit.

Finally I went to humor.

We had a Saturday-afternoon game on national television, and we were deep into the second half and I hadn't been to the line yet. Understand that, of all the Celtics, I drove to the basket more than anyone. So you might expect that I'd be fouled more than anyone else, right? But I hadn't even taken a free throw attempt in this game. At the next stoppage in play I went over to Sid.

"You know," I said, "this game's on national TV and I haven't seen my mother in two months. If you call a foul that gets me to the line, they'll do a nice big closeup of me and she'll be able to see that I'm okay."

He didn't say anything. He just walked away.

Now the play went down to the other end of the court and the guy who was guarding me had to be five feet away at least. I took one step, and he barely brushed me. Sid blew his whistle anyway. So we all traipsed over to the free throw line, and as I stood there, waiting to shoot, he flipped the ball to me and said, "Okay, that's it for your mother!"

And that *was* it; I didn't get another call the rest of the game.

There was a lot of humanity to Sid Borgia.

Jim Duffy was a guy you could talk with, too.

I could go up to him and say, "Hey, Duff, I don't know what's going on here, but do you realize that even though I drive to the hoop a lot, you haven't sent me to the line once tonight?" He'd say, "No kidding, Tommy." And I'd say, "No, I'm serious." Next thing you'd know, I'd be on the line.

You could appeal to some guys for justice.

Norm Drucker was another one I liked. One night I drove to the basket, attempted a shot, and was fouled. He blew his whistle and said: "Okay, Tommy, take a free throw." I asked, "Why just one?" He said, "Because you were passing off." I looked at him and said, "Normie, you know I never pass the ball!" We both laughed and he said, "Okay, take two."

But my favorite Norm Drucker story was the night he finally got exasperated with Walt Bellamy, a center who was in the league for fourteen years. Bellamy had a unique way of talking about himself; he always referred to himself in the third person. You'd hear him walking up the court saying: "Walter didn't do that. Walter didn't walk. Walter wasn't in there for three seconds. You never call a foul on Mr. Russell or Mr. Chamberlain. Why do you always call the foul on Walter?" He was forever complaining to the refs about every little thing.

Normie couldn't stand it any more. So he beckoned this big 6'11" guy to come over to where he was standing—Drucker, of course, was quite a bit shorter—and he made Bellamy lean down so that he could whisper up into his ear: "Tell *Walter* I just called a technical foul on him!"

*   *   *

Arnie Heft was another ref who had humanity.

We were playing Baltimore one night early in my career at the University of Maryland Field House, and he tossed me out of the game with two technicals. Later, as we were all leaving the locker room to catch a bus, Heft was outside waiting for me.

"Tommy," he said, "I hear you had your first son today."

"That's right."

"Well, I'll tell you what," he said. "If I turn in these technicals the league is going to fine you. So I won't turn them in, if you promise me something."

"What's that, Arnie?"

"Promise me you'll take that money and buy the kid a bond."

That's the kind of stuff that went on in those days.

Then there was Richie Powers. He and I had a thing going for years, because I always maintained he had a Napoleon complex. I mean, he *was* basketball. "You're not going to do that in *my* game," he'd say.

He once fouled me out of a playoff game in Los Angeles in something like sixteen or eighteen minutes, and of the 6 fouls that were assessed to me, 5 were originally called by the other official in my favor, only to be overturned by Richie, even though he was thirty feet away when he overturned them! I've still got a picture that shows me standing on the sidelines bitching at him that night.

He would do things like that to me all the time, and there was never any such thing as talking it over with him later, the way I did with Mendy. Richie just didn't like me, I'm afraid.

Now I was coaching and he was still in the league, and he and I still weren't hitting it off at all. We were in a playoff series with Philadelphia, and Richie called a technical on Jo Jo White, even though Jo Jo was under the basket at the other end of the court at the time. That sent me flying off the bench, demanding to know what Jo Jo did. Richie told me he thought he heard Jo Jo mumble something.

Now I was yelling: "Goddamn it, Richie, you're paranoid! You'd better get your ass to a shrink in a hurry."

Well . . . did that ever set off a time bomb! He went bananas: "You're out! Out! Out-out-out of the goddamn ball game! Right now. Go! You're outta here!"

I didn't find out until years later that he actually had been seeing a shrink at the time.

I guess he thought I knew.

But referees can blow you right out of a game with those whistles, so dealing with them is not all fun and laughter. Far from it.

The worst experience I ever had was in a playoff game I coached at Madison Square Garden in 1973, the year the Knicks won their second title. It was Game 4, and we were trailing in the series, 2–1. With ten minutes to go and Havlicek not even playing because of a shoulder injury, we had a 16-point lead. Then the New York crowd—they had 19,694 there that day—began chanting: "Dee-fense! Dee-fense!" The building shook with emotion, and the refs, Jack Madden and Jake O'Donnell, simply got caught up in it. The next seven calls went against us, and some were highly questionable, not to mention several noncalls against the Knicks for violations they were committing on inbounds plays and backcourt possessions.

It was awful and so out of whack it was bizarre; the ultimate coach's nightmare. The Knicks scored 13 points in a row and ended up beating us in double overtime. We went on to lose the series in seven.

Could just one whistle that afternoon have changed the course of championship history? Who knows? Looking back, it's certainly plausible.

*　　*　　*

Discrepancies in foul shots always bug a coach.

Sometimes it's just a matter of two refs with different philosophies and different interpretations of what constitutes a foul working opposite ends of the court. The guy who's under the basket at one end becomes the top official at the other end, and it's usually the guy underneath who's calling the fouls. So what you end up with are conflicting or inconsistent calls, and it's that inconsistency that causes most of the beefs.

That's why you always have to analyze the refs who are working your game. Auerbach did this every halftime, and warned us not to give any lip to an official he thought was likely to give us a break in the second half.

When you realize these guys hold your destiny in their hands, it's easy to become nonplussed, even hysterical, at times.

One ref—I won't mention his name—tossed me out of a game, and when I got a copy of the report he sent to the league I saw where he had written: "Heinsohn was acting like a meniak!" So I sent my copy of his report back to league headquarters, along with a blank check and a personal note: "When this guy learns how to spell 'maniac,' I'll pay the fine."

I will admit, however, that I did have my moments. One night, while wearing loafers, I tried to kick a towel. The loafer flew off my foot and sailed seventeen rows into the stands with a streamer attached— the towel had flown right along with it. Another night, when the refs had me moving around a lot, I bent down and split my pants: I mean *wide* open! So I had to stay on the bench the rest of the half, until our trainer could repair them with tape. That was probably the most embarrassing moment, though I also felt silly the night I threw my jacket in disgust and saw money, credit cards, everything in my pockets scatter all over the court. My Mobil card ended up down by the other basket.

So, yes, I was emotional. But I was never a *meniak!*

One thing no ref ever wants to hear you say is that he's not hustling. Nothing will get you into hot water quicker than telling him that.

Earl Strom is one of the referees I admire most. He's not a young man anymore, yet he's still out there calling good games and physically staying up with the play. But there was a period he went through where his legs were giving him trouble and he was often out of position. I didn't want to get on his case; I knew he was working hard. But what choice did I have? So he'd get upset, start screaming back at me, and the next thing I knew I was gone.

Yet I could see his point: "I'm out here doing my best with a pulled muscle and this guy is going to start giving me a hard time? No way, baby. I don't need his crap tonight."

So I have a suggestion.

I think basketball should do what hockey does: go to three officials, but limit two of them to calling three-second violations, inbounds infractions, goal-tending, zone defenses, things like that, the things that don't put you out of the game. Then have that third official stay at midcourt, moving no more than one or two steps in either direction, and let him call the personal fouls.

He'd be someone seasoned in the game, someone who'd gained the wisdom of Solomon through hands-on experience, someone who understood the difference between incidental contact and a harmful foul, someone who would not be swayed by the whims of the crowd. He'd be someone who'd guarantee an element of consistency, which is sorely needed.

The way it is now, as soon as a ref gains all of this needed maturity it's time for him to retire. But you could keep an Earl Strom until he was eighty with this system. You could keep a Darrell Garretson. You could keep anyone you wanted to keep. You certainly would have wanted to keep a Sid Borgia.

Sid Borgia, by the way, should be in the Hall of Fame. I wrote a letter to the Hall several years ago, urging his induction. He always showed great courage, great character. Besides, anyone who'd let a guy go to the foul line so that his mother could see he was okay deserves to be remembered with fondness.

That's how I'll remember Sid.

That's how I'll remember them all.

○ **18** ○
Sabotaged!

My greatest advantage as a coach was having Red Auerbach as my general manager, not only because we agreed on principles and philosophies, but also because he protected my rear. I never had to be concerned with looking over my shoulder at him, nor did he ever have to worry about where my loyalties lay. It was kind of like a son joining his father in the family business. We had our piddling differences, but the family business was going well, having added the 1976 championship to the one we won in 1974.

But Bob Schmertz, our owner, died in the summer of 1975; and once his partner, Irv Levin, acquired control of the team from his estate and personally assumed command, nothing was ever the same again.

The ultimate bottom-line guy, the consummate meddler, Levin proceeded to involve himself at every level of the organization, interfering with communication at every level, refusing to leave day-to-day control of the operation in the hands of a management team that had enjoyed a long, proven record of success.

He was a multimillionaire who concerned himself

with the wasteful disposition of used typewriter ribbons, and it was that kind of pettiness that soon spread anxiety throughout the rank and file. His insidious heavy-handedness brought about a total breakdown of corporate morale. When an owner starts talking with the players, the coach is in trouble. When an owner starts talking with the coach, the GM is in trouble. With Levin, we were all in trouble.

One thing was inviolate about the way the Celtics operated. I never talked with an owner unless Red was there, and Red never talked with my players unless I was there or he asked me first. It was just the way we did business, the way we both liked it. We found it eliminated a lot of problems. We trusted each other.

But the GM can't be guarding the coach's back when he has to keep looking over his shoulder to guard his own, and this is what began to happen.

Levin always wanted to meet with me and meet with the players, when the team was on the road. He started taking road trips with us. When we played in California, his home, he wanted us to attend a party so he could show off for his friends. I refused, which didn't go over well. It was supposed to have been a command performance, I guess, but it just wasn't the way I was used to doing business.

Red had always been successful in keeping owners away from the team, but Levin wasn't receptive to his thoughts on the subject. In fact, Red was starting to feel pressure of his own. Levin was forever calling him, trying to get him to go on the road, which Red had stopped doing years earlier, except for special games and playoffs. It was obvious what was happening. Once Levin got a look at the payroll and saw Auerbach's salary, which was the highest of any GM in the league, he figured he could save a chunk of dough by getting rid of Red. But he was smart enough to know you don't come right out and fire a guy like

Red in a city where he's revered. You just frustrate him as much as you can, and bide your time.

Looking back at the way things turned out, it's clear now that I made a mistake. Red never tells anybody everything. He plays his cards close to the vest. I should have been quicker on the uptake; I should have sensed he was in trouble, too. But I didn't, and I don't know why, because we had weathered a similar storm back when I first started to coach, when an absentee ownership out of New York, on the verge of bankruptcy, wanted to oust Red and give his job to Dick Lynch, the former Giants football player.

I discovered this plan when Red sent me to scout the NIT and told me to meet with them while I was there, to find out what was on their minds. I found out, all right, when Lynch pulled me aside and proceeded to pitch me about becoming the "head basketball guy" when he took over as general manager.

I made a beeline for Auerbach's office.

"Red," I said, "do you know what's going on here?"

"Yeah, I know. Tommy, I'm not getting along too well with these guys. I think I might leave. I've got an offer from Philadelphia."

"Whoa," I said. "If you go to Philly, I want to go with you." If this ownership didn't want Auerbach, I didn't want them.

Eventually they went under, and things went back to normal.

I should have done the same thing as soon as it became obvious that Levin was bad news. If Red and I had been more unified, if we had been working from the same page, things might have turned out differently. But once Red's security was threatened, my security was threatened, and things got worse in a hurry.

After we won the 1976 championship, which Levin

arrived in time to enjoy, the makeup of the team changed drastically.

Paul Silas had to be traded after someone left a loophole in his contract, which not only took away an essential player, but also did a tune on Dave Cowens's head. Silas had taken a lot of the rebounding load off Dave, who did not relish the prospect of now having to fight that battle alone.

Cowens also did a dumb thing that summer. Instead of taking time to rest and to recharge his batteries after having virtually carried us on his back to the title, he went to Japan to give a series of clinics, then came home to run his camp and remained constantly on the go, fulfilling all kinds of commitments. When he reported to us that fall, he was already out of gas. Emotions were essential to Dave's game; he used to intimidate people with his emotions. Now they were drained, and as soon as he started trying to hack it without Silas, he couldn't respond anymore. So he took a walk for thirty games in the middle of that season, a total burnout, like Dick Vermeil said he was when he quit as coach of the Philadelphia Eagles.

Sidney Wicks and Curtis Rowe, neither of whom were our kind of players—and both of whom eventually became persona non grata with the team and the public—were added to the roster late that fall and, for better or worse, we were on our way.

Given all that was going on—Cowens taking his sabbatical; veterans slowing down, but not wanting to leave; morale problems among players who began going directly to Levin with their complaints—I thought I did my best job of coaching that season, especially in the playoffs, when, as Hubie Brown would have put it, we took Philadelphia to seven.

So I went to Maine and fell off a cliff, which is what you do when you've just been knocked out of the playoffs and you've still got all this emotion running through your body; you're still pushing, still running on adrenaline. You go away, and it's like falling off a cliff. My way of doing that was to go to Maine and get lost in painting. That's what I had been doing for three or four days when I picked up a Boston paper and read a story that asked: "Will Tommy Heinsohn be back?"

I couldn't believe it. After the job I had just done? There had to be a mistake. So I went to a pay phone and called the office.

"Red," I asked, "is there some problem about me coaching this ballclub?"

"Tommy," he said, "you'd better come home. We've gotta talk."

We met the next afternoon in a North End restaurant and it was a very unpleasant session.

Red began by putting me on the defensive, by challenging me on coaching techniques, like attacking the way I conducted my practices.

"Look," he said, "I've been talking with some of the players and . . ."

"What? You've been talking to the players? You promised me you'd *never* talk to the players without going through me first!"

Now I was upset and angry, and I guess he knew it, because he tried explaining how it had happened. I didn't even hear him.

"Red," I said, steaming, "are you trying to tell me I don't know what I'm doing? Okay, I'm not as great as you were. I understand that. But goddamn it, I won two championships with the smallest team in the league. I won with a 6'8" center, who then goes off the deep end because the organization lets Silas get away by screwing up his contract! But I didn't say a word about that, did I? No. I just gave the writers the ol' bullshit about how it was a deal that had to be made, even though we both know it ripped the goddamn guts out of my club! Ol' Tommy covered the company's ass on that one, didn't he?"

It was true. That's how Silas got away, the same way Paul Westphal got away before him: A few i's weren't dotted, a few t's weren't crossed. We're talking major-league screwups here. That's why Red brought in Jan Volk, who's general manager now. Jan's great at contracts. The people Red had doing them before messed up badly.

So I spoke my piece over lunch that day, and, looking back, I'd say I missed the boat. Red was wrong for the way he approached me. That was his mistake. And my mistake was failing to pick up his signals, failing to suspect that he was making me insecure because someone had already made him insecure. He practically admitted as much when he said,"You know, Levin's been calling me an awful lot." But I was so damn mad I missed it. What I should have said was, "Hey, Red, are you in trouble?"

I wish I had.

The following week the two of us met with Levin to discuss the team's future and my own.

Levin asked me what I thought needed to be done, and I told him it was time to think about rebuilding, which is not what he wanted to hear, because he was of the opinion he'd bought a championship team. He must have told me a dozen times: "We've got eight All-Stars!"

"Irv," I said, "you're right. Okay? We do have guys who were All-Stars—but they're not All-Stars now. Let me tell you something. In the years I played here and in the years I've coached here, whenever we've had our greatest success the question marks were always the eighth and ninth men on the team. Never the nucleus. But now the questions revolve around our nucleus. John Havlicek is thirty-seven years old. What kind of season is he going to give us when he's thirty-eight? Dave Cowens disappeared for three months. Where will his head be at next year? Sidney Wicks. Are you going to sign Sidney again? What about Jo Jo? Are you going to sign Jo Jo? And do you know that after Charlie Scott broke his arm, doctors told him if he breaks it in the same spot again they may have to amputate?''

I urged him to trade Curtis Rowe and to get us a guard, which we badly needed. And I reminded him that Wicks, who had been a significant contributor, was up for a new contract. "I can't guarantee you Sidney will give us the same effort once he gets a new deal," I said."So if you think it's too much money to spend, I'll give you a list of five guys who could replace him." And I did: I already had a list made up of names like Harvey Catchings.

I also told him, "You've got every right, as owner, to talk with the players, but I would certainly appreciate being there."

That got no response at all.

He stood up, as if to signify that the meeting was over, and said, "Listen, I don't want any excuses, okay? Just get the damn job done."

Then he gave me a two-year contract and I headed back to Maine.

The bottom began to fall out as soon as training camp opened.

Havlicek had his appendix taken out and didn't show up until the final three days. Jo Jo and his agent agreed on a deal with Red, but then Levin reneged and now Jo Jo was sulking all over the place, which got the other players mad at him because they figured he was a malcontent. Levin fought with Wicks over a contract throughout the camp, and now everybody in town was getting on Sidney's ass because it was made to appear he was holding out. And they didn't sign Sidney Wicks until three hours before the opening game, though I had pleaded to get him signed early so that he and Cowens could finally have a training camp together.

That was the picture confronting me as we got under way. No Havlicek. No Wicks. No trades. No new backup guard.

Then Cowens, who'd had the head problem the year before, comes up to me and says, "I want to go on a Nautilus program, so I'll probably miss practice every other day."

This was the guy I was counting on to replace Havlicek as my team leader. I'd already lost Havlicek over Jo Jo. Besides, John was getting ready to retire, and frankly he was more interested in going out with his big Day than he was in rebuilding the club. It wasn't John's job to lead us anymore. It was up to Cowens to take on that responsibility.

I went to Red and asked him to talk with Dave.

"Tommy," he said, "you know he's had these problems, and we don't want to put too much pressure on him. . . ."

So that was it. Cowens got his way.

That was probably another mistake on my part. I should have done with Dave what I did with Havlicek, Don Nelson, and Satch Sanders the first year I coached. I sat down with them and said: "Look, you guys know as much basketball as I do, and it'll be a lot easier dealing with these new guys if we're all coming from the same direction, if they hear the same things from you that they're going to be hearing from me. We'll get where we all want to go a lot faster that way." I asked them to help me lead, and they did.

I should have done the same thing with Cowens, but I allowed myself to be dissuaded when Red said, "Let's not chance it," and that was my fault. Knowing the way he responds to challenges, I might have had a renewed Cowens; and boy, we sure could have used that.

We were anything but an all-together team as we broke camp. After getting torn apart in most of our exhibition games, we opened the season with three losses in a row on the road, then won one game and lost our next five. The die was cast early. We were going nowhere, and, worst of all, we knew it.

* * *

The beautiful part of playing, and of coaching—assuming you're in the right situation—is that you make a decision, then act, then see the results right away. The shot goes in or it doesn't go in. The play works or it doesn't work. You act, then suffer the consequences. But when the fear of those consequences becomes all-pervading, you don't act at all. You do nothing.

This is a big problem in the business world. Businesspeople are so concerned with protecting their turf that they try to put off making decisions as long as they can, and the ones they do make cause them a great deal of agony because the results of their acts may not be perceived in a positive light for weeks or months. So they become political people, learning ways to protect themselves until those acts bear fruit.

I was never a politician in all my years with the Celtics, neither as a player nor as a coach. Maybe it was naiveté on my part, but I always abdicated the position of protecting myself to Red. I didn't worry about it. I left that for him to handle, and he always did—until Levin came along, making his own position very shaky, very tenuous.

That's when I paid the price for being politically naive. When I was left on my own to fend for myself, I didn't know how to do it.

As the season continued to fall apart, so did whatever remained of our morale.

Levin was taking key guys—Havlicek, Jo Jo, Cowens—to dinner behind my back at the Algonquin club, welcoming their complaints, and there were plenty of unhappy guys on that team. No coach keeps everyone happy, even in the best of situations. Now that unhappiness was fortified by an owner who offered a sympathetic ear.

I was still coach, but I was no longer in control.

Red felt control slipping away, too, like the day only two players showed up for the family Christmas party, which he considered a cherished Celtic tradition. That really hurt him, though by then he knew there was major trouble in paradise.

Earlier that month Portland came into the Garden and creamed us by 31 points. The fans were booing. It was awful. Auerbach and Levin came storming out of the stands, across the court, and into the locker room, where Red pulled me aside. "Tommy," he said, "I want to talk to these guys."

He proceeded to give a Red Auerbach speech, but unlike the old days, when he would use names, usually mine and Loscy's, he thought he'd play it safe and name positions: "Now you forwards, you aren't doing this. And you guards . . ." He mentioned no one specifically, but when he was halfway through his review of the guards, Jo Jo stood up, still in uniform, grabbed his clothes, said, "I quit!" and stalked out.

I called Red the next morning. "What should we do, fine him?" I asked.

"No, no, Tommy," he says. "I'll take care of it. I'll talk to him. Don't worry."

Jo Jo missed practice for the next couple of days while Red tried to cajole him into returning. He had been the playoff MVP two years earlier and considered himself the consummate Celtic. But when he and his agent agreed to terms with Red, only to have Levin start nickel-and-diming him, they lost his head. Now they'd lost his heart, too. He came back, but he never gave a damn about the team anymore.

Right after that episode there was a luncheon held by some group in town. I spoke. Red spoke. Then Levin got up, and in the course of his remarks he began making offhand comments about the job I was doing. It was awkward and embarrassing, but I let it pass.

Then, just before the start of that Christmas party that most of the team boycotted, I received a call from a *New York Times* stringer who was wondering what I thought of Levin asking Red to return to the bench. Talk about a bombshell! I said, "That's news to me," and then went right to Red's office.

"Red, what the hell is going on here? Has he offered you my job?"

"Well, Tommy . . . blah, blah, blah."

He never gave me an answer. But he sure looked unhappy.

The answer came a few mornings later as I arrived at practice to find Auerbach and Levin waiting for me.

"Tommy," Red said, as Levin stood by listening, "sit over there for a minute, will you?"

Then he gathered the team around him and changed all my plays.

He knew what that would do to me, and though I have no doubt he was doing it at Levin's bidding, he was nevertheless doing it at my expense.

They destroyed me that morning.

What Levin was hoping to do was embarrass me into quitting so that he wouldn't have to honor my contract. I knew exactly what he was up to, but as I sat there watching them make a fool out of me I said to myself, "Baby, if you're gonna do this to me, you're gonna pay for the fuckin' privilege!"

They'd have to fire me. I wasn't going to make it easy for them.

They were nice enough to wait until after the holidays—a little warmth on their part. Then, the morning of January 3, I showed up early for a ten o'clock practice and Red was already there. "Tommy," he said, "you know this is very uncomfortable for me, but it's not working out. We're going to have to let you go. I got a call from Levin last night. . . ."

As soon as I heard that I knew there was no point in discussing the matter any further. So I said, "See you later, Red," and walked out the door.

*　　*　　*

I was forty-four years old. I had been the Celtics coach for almost nine years, nearly as long as I had been a Celtics player.

After they fired me I sat around the house for almost a year, doing nothing, caring about nothing. All of my juices were dried. All of my energies were gone. I'm a very enthusiastic guy—my enthusiasm is a very precious commodity to me—and now it seemed I was unable to get enthused about anything else in my life. I had spent all of my enthusiasm on the Boston Celtics, and it would be at least a year before I felt like a whole human being again.

One of my regrets is that I wasn't around to personally witness the end of the Irv Levin era, the public vilification that chased him out of town. I missed it by three months. But I was still following the stories in the papers and I had to laugh at the way it happened.

It was the classic Auerbach setup.

The Celtics had asked Havlicek if there was anything special he wanted from them on John Havlicek Day, which was scheduled for the final day of the regular season. I'm sure Levin planned to present him with a watch or a plaque or maybe some used typewriter ribbons. A magnanimous gesture was clearly in order, and somehow or other it was ascertained that the magnanimous gesture Havlicek preferred was a camper that cost in the vicinity of $40,000!

I can just picture Red trying to convince Levin that this wonderful display of generosity on his part was sure to be well-respected by the fans, who were very unhappy about the way things were going. And I can picture Levin telling himself: "Ah, hell, maybe he's right. Maybe it's worth it. The fans can't help but love me when I hand the keys to Havlicek."

So he forked over the dough for the camper, and when the big moment arrived he strutted to midcourt, keys in hand, fully anticipating the resounding ovation Auerbach had told him he'd be sure to receive. But the minute the PA man announced his name, the crowd booed his ass right out of the ceremony!

He was humiliated, with no place to hide except next to Red, who was cheered as if he'd just won another title.

Talk about Porky's Revenge!

I think that was the moment Irv Levin finally realized this was Red Auerbach's town, because when the next season rolled around he was just a bad memory in Boston.

I had many offers to coach again, most of which I rejected out of hand. I just wasn't up to giving anyone else what I had given the Celtics. I listened to a couple of proposals, and they were flattering, but the enthusiasm was still gone.

Then the Houston Rockets called in 1983, before they gave the job to Bill Fitch. Would I at least come down to hear what they had to say? Would I at least talk with them?

I told Ray Patterson, the GM there, "I'm not averse to listening, but, really, I'm happy with my life in Boston."

At his urging I flew down with my agent, Phil McLaughlin, and they talked to us about a bonus plan and living expenses, and a salary equal to the highest in the league. But money was never the issue with me. When they added it all up, it amounted to less than I was already making in the business world. Money wasn't going to woo me there. What I wanted to know was how much control I'd have, and would we all be on the same wavelength?

I decided to test that as we talked, telling Patterson that one of the first players I'd want him to go after would be Ronnie Lee, not because Ronnie was a super talent, but because I knew we'd have super practices with him. Baby, when you played against Ronnie Lee, you went back to your locker room and counted your fingers and toes. That's how hard he'd work you. But you had to be a basketball person to know what he could mean to a team.

Patterson looked at me like I was nuts; and, though we kept talking, that's when the interview ended.

I was actually relieved as we boarded the flight to Boston because, for just a little while there as we talked about the game, I thought I felt those juices beginning to stir. But now, heading home, I was sure I had made the right decision.

So when the stewardess came by and asked if I wanted a glass of champagne, I told her, "Sweetheart, I just turned down a million dollars, and I'm so damn happy—why don't you bring the bottle!"

° **19** °

Hold the Presses!

There was a time in this country when the written word was the primary source of information, so the press had a tremendous impact on sports. Even when radio came along with its great play-by-play men like Bill Stearns, newspapers still were the dominant shapers of public opinion. When Grantland Rice, trying to fashion an image for his readers, described the Notre Dame backfield as the Four Horsemen of the Apocalypse, he created a piece of literature that's still revered today.

I've often thought that if the press of those days had been anything like the press we see now, Babe Ruth never would have emerged as a hero and Franklin Delano Roosevelt probably wouldn't have been elected president.

Reporters were more inclined to report the event back then, rather than their own interpretations of what they saw; and they didn't feel compelled to pry into the personal lives of the individuals they were covering. We were still a society more or less coming out of the Victorian era, and a lot of things remained in the closet. We were still a society with some restraints; even reporters felt them.

I'm no press historian, but my understanding is that

this was the mood when the country was young, when it wasn't quite as established as it is now, when it was a melting pot of immigrants who kept arriving in great numbers, an amalgam of many cultures and backgrounds looking for a common identity, looking for the country that was paved with gold—looking for *heroes.*

Sports, no matter what civilization you're talking about, have always been an integral part of a people's culture, whether it was the Greeks with their marathons, the Romans with their gladiators, or whatever. Every country had its heroes, so why shouldn't America? So we developed our own games: baseball, then football. These were celebrated as "our" games, and their best players became "our" heroes. Now we had our own stars, and the early role of the press was to give the people what they wanted: stars and heroes!

Sports were something everyone could have in common; you talked sports. One of my favorite childhood memories is picturing my father glued to the radio after the war, listening to the World Series. Somehow sports made you feel better about the world. That was even truer during the hard times of the Great Depression, when sports were seen as a microcosm of life, showing how you could bounce back if you really tried.

That's what sold papers: creating stars, not tearing them down. No one was looking for little chinks in the armor. There was almost a reluctance to write derogatorily unless something was so blatant, so criminal, like the Black Sox scandal, that it couldn't be ignored.

So Babe Ruth became a great American hero, and if he had any immoral inclinations they were dismissed as eccentricities. He was the *Bambino,* visiting kids in hospitals and promising them he'd hit home runs. A PR guy wouldn't dare suggest a scenario like that today. But that's what the public wanted to believe. It wanted these virtues in its heroes, so the press never bothered to mention that the Bambino was also a glutton and a drunk. Heroes had no flaws; that's what made them heroes. Besides, what difference did it make? He was still the Sultan of Swat, wasn't he? If he had eaten fewer hot dogs, what would it have meant—*five* more homers?

Today they count every hot dog. Not only would the Babe have found steamy details of his peccadilloes splattered across front pages, but he also would have found columnists writing: "Look, if this slob hadn't eaten all those extra hot dogs he might have hit five more home runs."

When I arrived in Boston as a rookie in 1956, the notion of "heroes" was still around but slipping fast. Dave Egan, the city's best-read sports columnist, had set the stage for all the writers who followed him by taking on Ted Williams in a personal feud they shared for years. Ted was the ultimate star—not just a legendary hitter, but a bona fide war hero, too—and now here came "the Colonel," which is what they called Egan, to tell the world that the *Splendid Splinter* was really a louse! Egan hated Williams. Williams hated Egan. It created great ammunition for discussing sports—and it also sold papers.

Egan was as much of a revolutionary in his game as Cousy or Russell were in mine because he helped to change the way his game was played. Once it became established that you could sell even more papers by being against something, a new era was born because the overall aim of any newspaper is to sell more papers. This is what you have to remember about newspapers: It's a business venture with a bottom line, and the bottom line is to find out what sells and deliver it as often as you can.

Then something else came along to change the way newspapers covered sports. That something else was television.

Televison, with one picture, could convey in an instant what a columnist needed hundreds of words to describe. By editing, by selecting just the right frame and just the right phrase, television could tell a whole story in a fleeting moment. So people began turning to television for their news. It was an easier way to acquire information.

Now the printed medium, finding itself in competition with a visual medium, had a major challenge: *What could people read in a newspaper that they couldn't see on TV? What could papers tell them that they didn't already know?* For newspapers, this became the essence of survival; the skill of the writer became paramount. Advancements in technology have only increased the pressure to come up with something new, something titillating, something saleable. By the time the fan goes to bed now he already knows the score, he's probably seen footage of the critical plays, and he has most likely heard the athletes sharing their innermost thoughts.

How is a newspaper supposed to compete with that? There were seven Boston papers when I was a rookie. Today there are two. And that's been the trend all over the country since TV changed the way Americans get their news.

But television wasn't the only factor affecting the way newspapers approached sports.

There's a generation of writers now in their thirties and forties who were taught in their adolescent years that it was not only okay, it was *fashionable* to question authority. They grew up reading about marches and protests and sit-ins and antiwar demonstrations, and they saw for themselves that nothing garnered more attention, nothing sold more papers, than negative news. They learned, by observation if not by experience, that a bullish market existed for anyone who was angry and knew how to express it.

So, when members of this generation began moving into the field of sportswriting, they brought with them a natural cynicism, an unwillingness to assume that anything could be as decent or as innocent as it appeared. There *had* to be something wrong somewhere; all you had to do was look hard enough for it.

So sports became gossipy. The best illustration is Pete Vecsey, who's made a nice career for himself by living off the NBA's grapevine. His "notes" columns in the *New York Post* are more popular and better-read than any game stories in the country.

Yet game stories underwent a great change when this new generation of writers came along. A good example occurred in Boston.

Bob Ryan, who still writes for the *Boston Globe*, took over the Celtics beat for that paper during my rookie year as coach. He was twenty-three, fresh out of college, and he'd grown up watching basketball, much the way the writers who covered teams I'd played on had grown up watching baseball and hockey. Ryan was a fan, and he wrote with a flair. Fans could identify with him, and he began providing them with little insights, little bits of inside stuff, along with his own opinions of whom he liked and didn't like, what he liked and didn't like.

If you followed basketball you read what Ryan had to say. I don't think people particularly cared what his counterpart, Eddie Gillooly of the *Record-American* and later the *Herald-American,* had to say, even though Eddie was a much better news guy. He certainly broke more big stories than Ryan did; but he didn't do it with great pizzazz, and there was nothing subjective about his style. Eddie was simply an old pro, someone who reported the facts.

Ryan, meanwhile, quickly came to think of himself as a basketball guru. His game stories became little more than collections of his own opinions. He'd come into the locker room before writing his stories, and I'd be given the opportunity to confirm or deny what-

176

ever conclusions he'd already reached. I was the coach, but he no longer asked for, or apparently needed, *my* observations. His postgame interviews became predictable. He would state a premise, explaining how *he* had viewed the game, what *he* thought it had been all about, and then I would be allowed to say either yes or no. That was the only input he needed from me. I would nod my head one way or the other, and that was the extent of my participation.

He got lost in his ego. He became bigger, in his own mind, than either the game or the team he was covering, to a point where he was no longer as interested in covering the Celtics as he was in promoting Bobby Ryan. The name of his game was now self-aggrandizement, and even when he started to *coach* the club in his stories I could overlook his zeal. But when it got to the point where it was divisive, where it was detrimental to my team, then he and I had a very serious problem.

If he had covered the Celtics when Auerbach was coaching, Red would have slapped him down in a minute. But that wasn't my nature. I was more inclined to work with these guys, to take them out for lunch, to spend time with them, and to make myself available to them. They all had my home phone number. I tried to make their jobs easier, not that I felt it would win me anything; I just saw it as part of my job.

Aggressive media can help a team.

But they can also destroy a team by wrecking its morale.

Ryan became friends with several of the players, some of whom conned him into writing things they wanted to see in the paper because they had axes to grind. They were using him, and he was encouraging them to do it.

No basketball team is a happy family. In any family there are bound to be some animosities; someone's always mad at someone else, maybe because he didn't get to use the bathroom first. That's what goes on all the time within any team. On any particular day one guy is apt to be mad at another guy, and if a writer is predisposed to zeroing in on all these petty jealousies, which are really no more than sibling rivalries, he's missing the larger point, which is that the entire family is nevertheless functioning well.

Ryan started thinking of himself as another member of our family, a participant in these intimate discussions in which two of the kids would talk about how mad they were at a third as if it were a world-shaking matter, when all it really came down to was more of "Who got into the bathroom first?" And when the children began seeing their gripes in print they liked it, too, because it gave their complaints the appearance of being legitimate. So now they were only too happy to tell him how mad they also were at Daddy.

I was Daddy.

It got ridiculous after a while. Here's a sample of what Ryan wrote the morning of Game 2 in our 1976 championship series against Phoenix—when we won our sixteenth championship and my second title as a coach: "Heinsohn is not a professional coach. He is a reasonably astute ex-player who has had seven years of on-the-job training. His managerial experience was in the insurance business; he had never coached anything in his life. Too bad such a great team isn't being led by someone displaying a little more grace under pressure."

That was quite a mouthful for someone who, just one year earlier in the acknowledgments section of a book he authored, thanked "Tom Heinsohn, whose friendliness and interest in a young reporter was most helpful and gratifying."

I felt abused, sure, but personal hurts aren't the real problem a coach faces when his unhappy players latch onto a stooge in the press. It's not the fact his ego has been bruised that upsets him so much, because he understands that it comes with the territory. The real problem is that he's losing an important tool of coaching when his credentials as a leader are trashed—because players read the papers, too.

Coaching's not like art, where all you need is a canvas and some paint, and where the goal can be strictly your personal satisfaction, which doesn't require anyone else's approval. I didn't need Ryan's approval to enjoy my job. But when he began making it difficult for me to perform that job by mocking my credentials in the eyes of my players, he became more than a nuisance; he became a monster for the entire organization.

The most pilloried coach in all of sports is probably John Thompson, the basketball coach at Georgetown.

I admire that guy so much because, in an effort to have his players experience life as college students rather than as stars, he allows himself to be attacked by writers, when the easiest thing in the world for him to do would be to provide them with whatever athletes they want for their stories.

But he won't do that, so reporters hate him. They say he's "uncooperative." But what's their primary reason for being mad at him? They're mad because he doesn't make their jobs easy. To me, that is the very thing that makes him special in an era when most major college programs spend *beaucoup* bucks catering to writers.

This guy goes the other way. He sets himself up as the scapegoat, sacrificing his own PR for the good of his kids because he wants them to be good *students* as well as good athletes, and he knows that all the media hoopla these writers bring with them will only serve to undermine that objective.

To me, that's a lofty goal, and it's a shame the way the media refuse to acknowledge what's behind their vendetta. Rather than being excoriated, John Thompson ought to be emulated. He's a standup guy, the kind of guy I'd have loved to have had coaching my own kids.

The bottom line, I'm afraid, is that most reporters no longer believe that pleasant stories work, or maybe it's just that they don't trust their own ability to tell those stories in a way that will intrigue their readers. So, to play it safe, they go on scavenger hunts for something sensational, something with a *bite*.

Look at Gary Hart. I wasn't a supporter of his, but that's immaterial. What did the problems that man had in his personal life have to do with his potential to be a good president? There's many a successful man who's lived the same kind of private life.

The Gary Hart story to me was pure American journalism: Build a guy up to be the consummate hero, which none of us are, then tear him apart when you find a flaw, which all of us have.

There's no such thing as the perfect human being, just like there's no such thing as the perfect basketball team, and if that's what we're looking for in our search for the right president, then we ought to call off the search right now, because there's no such animal.

Yet the media seem determined to impose a *Perfect Human Being Litmus Test* on people in public life—athletes, entertainers, political leaders—as if they could just stick someone's finger into a special chemical and then draw infallible conclusions by watching for the color that comes out: Red? We find him acceptable. Green? He's a goner.

It's no wonder a lot of good people choose not to offer themselves for public service in this country. The really tragic part of it all is that quite often these are people who are eminently qualified and want to serve for all the right reasons. But when they see what we do to public figures in this country, they just say no thanks, there's no way they're going to subject themselves or their families to that kind of abuse. Who needs it? And they're right.

We're all the losers when that happens.

*   *   *

People in public life understand that they have to answer to the media. That's the way the system works, and that's good.

But who do the media have to answer to?

Tell me how a newspaper in Phoenix feels free to publish the names of three NBA players who were mentioned in the presumed secrecy of a grand jury hearing? If the person who leaked those names to the paper was caught, he'd be guilty of a crime. So why isn't that newspaper just as guilty of subverting the intent of the law, which is to protect the reputations of people who might be innocent? If the person who released that information was guilty of a crime, why isn't the paper that profits from that crime equally guilty, or at least an accessory?

It reminded me of when the editors of the *New York Times* decided among themselves that it was okay to publish the Pentagon Papers. They saw no potential security risks in doing that. Who the hell elected them?

I'm sure this sounds like the sour grapes of someone who's had a bad experience with the media. That's not it at all. With very few exceptions, I've gotten along well with most of the reporters I've met in my life.

I'm just convinced there ought to be more fairness in what they do. Almost every other profession has to operate within guidelines or regulations aimed at assuring the public of competency. Here's a profession that can destroy reputations and bring down governments, yet it answers to no one.

What I'd love to see the media display is a little more of the ethics they seem to find lacking in everyone else.

Even if it doesn't sell as well.

° 20 °

The CBS Murder Mysteries

Every basketball game is a novel, a murder mystery. You know someone's going to be killed at the end, you just don't know who's going to do it and how it's going to be done.

When CBS hired me to be the analyst on its NBA telecasts, beginning with the 1983–84 season, my mandate, as I understood it, was to get the intrigue of each game, all the little nuances, across to the viewers, to get their minds working along with their rooting interests. We wanted to increase viewers' understanding of the battles of style and wit that were taking place before their eyes, to get them thinking along with the players and coaches and yet not in such a way that you had to be a devout aficionado to follow what was being said.

It was a large undertaking, and an appealing one.

Basketball's not an easy game to broadcast. For one thing, its rhythms change from game to game, so there's no set way of presenting it. Those rhythms can even change from minute to minute, quarter to quarter; they can change while the teams are in their huddles.

Football's different. You can tailor a pattern of broadcasting in football because you know you're going to have twenty-five or thirty seconds to say what you want after every play, without fear of having to edit yourself. And baseball's a different animal altogether; it's virtually a nonstop-talk sport because the action is so limited. But in basketball, with the ball changing hands so frequently and going from end to end on a moment's notice, you often have only two or three seconds to impart the grand strategy of World War III as you see it developing.

Notwithstanding those constraints, the CBS people were determined to get more of the game's strategies into each telecast. That's why I was brought aboard.

Until that time their approach to covering basketball was to focus on the high-fliers, on the marquee personalities, showing nothing but spectacular plays. They never allowed the game to speak for itself. The analysts they had—Oscar Robertson, Rick Barry, Jack Twyman, Keith Erickson, John Havlicek, and even Bill Russell—did little to dissuade the viewer of a common misconception that basketball is nothing more than a bunch of guys running up and down the floor in underwear, tossing a ball through a fishnet. They all understood certain elements of the game; but, with the exception of Russell, none of them had ever approached it from a coach's level, from the level of a general who must dissect each maneuver. They had all been captains only in the field.

I know that in the years I coached I never felt TV did justice to the sport.

Now they gave the microphone to me.

But I was the new guy, the outsider, and when you're dealing with network people you're dealing with very creative people, people with strong personalities, people who've made it to the top of a very competitive industry and have brought with them pre-conceived notions and hard-to-break habits. Here I was, potentially putting them into positions of exposing their own limited understanding of the game, and, let's face it, no one likes to appear ignorant.

Yet I'm a strong personality, too. I believed some of those habits and notions had to change, and I knew what could be done. It meant, for instance, changing the habits of a cameraman, as in changing the location of his camera. You're at the mercy of the man with the camera—you can't be talking about things that aren't in the picture—and yet he's a creative person, too, so you don't want to get his nose out of joint.

Forget the people at the top, the executives who issue memos and directives and give a network its corporate face. The people you need a relationship with are the people down there in the trenches, like the people who hold the cameras. It has to become a team effort, with each member of the team having faith in the abilities and judgments of the others and having confidence that the other guy is going to hold up his end.

It was a building process, and it was frustrating. At the end of the first year I almost quit. I thought to myself: "If they're not committed to this thing, then they don't need me. They need a Henny Youngman, someone who'll feed them a lot of one-liners." I seriously thought about resigning at that point. There are many funnier people than me around; Johnny Kerr, an ex-coach with a lot of expertise, is another Bob Uecker. I just didn't think that was the best of what I could be in a broadcast booth.

It took time—I had to take something off my fastball while they had to let down their guards—but gradually we began to have a meeting of the minds. The battle lines that had been drawn—"Are we supposed to be *entertaining,* or are we supposed to be *infor-*

mative?''—began to recede. In time they all but disappeared as we began to realize we could be both.

The games I used to watch while I was coaching indicated there was no concept of trying to incorporate a team's style of play into the telecast.

That was very much on my mind when I took the job.

Cameramen, for example, used to show rebounders from the shoulders up, trying to get the ball into the picture. I told them: "Put the bottom of the net at the top of the frame, so that it's just visible, and forget the ball. If it goes through we'll all know it, because we'll see it dropping through the net. What we want to capture is all of the action that's going on while the ball is up in the air—the hooking, the tripping, the banging of legs, everything! That's the *action* of basketball! You're showing the rebound action from when the ball hits the rim. Hell, when the ball hits the rim, the action's over."

We began to show the furious fighting that takes place when guys are trying to establish good rebounding positions.

It was like art to me. We started out with the broad brush strokes, or the basic concepts of rebounding, of shooting, of defense, of a fast break. Then once those broad brush strokes were applied—things as basic as "There are nine pounds of air in the ball"—we went to work on the finer details: "Why isn't that fast break working? What's the defense doing to stop it?"

I never liked seeing a camera follow the ball. Who needs a closeup of a spinning ball? I'd tell them, "The basketball is the magician's empty hand," meaning that while that ball is up in the air, something significant is happening somewhere else.

The Lakers' fast break was a great example.

The way Pat Riley has his guys trained, they won't let the ball hit the floor once after the other team has scored, if it's at all possible; the point of that is to cut down on the reaction time you allow the defense. To me, this is informative; it's an item of interest. So we'd have a camera fixed on Kurt Rambis, showing him grabbing the ball as it went through the net, stepping out of bounds, then whipping an outlet pass to trigger the break. Before the shooter had even released his shot, the Lakers knew from habit and from watching where Rambis was positioned, where they were going.

We showed this through pictures, describing the strategy as it unfolded on the screen; and in doing that we not only increased the viewers' appreciation of the Lakers' great technique, we also created an image for Rambis.

That's what we did: We painted pictures.

While Dick Stockton, the play-by-play man, would be painting a picture of a guy who was good to his mother, I'd be coming in with examples of why he was great as a basketball player: "James Worthy is great for this LA team because there's nobody in the league who gets out and forms a three-man attack any faster than he does. He's always putting heat on the defense." And we'd show that in a picture.

We'd show the quickness of an Akeem Olajuwon, explaining how devastating that could be to opposing centers; we'd show the way Isiah Thomas *pushed* the ball upcourt against a defense; we'd show how Spud Webb defied the bigger guys with pure speed.

We'd have our own team meetings—producers, directors, cameramen, technicians, Stockton, me—as we planned for each game, and in an effort to correctly anticipate what that game might offer in the way of a story line and special themes, I'd prepare a scouting report on each team, just as if I were getting a team of my own ready to play them. I'd envision myself as the opposing coach, trying to project where the battle was going to be fought and who was going to establish the style. Then we'd attempt to translate that into specific pictures, so that the viewers would be able to *see* the strategies I was trying to describe.

Ultimately, what we wanted to do was have our viewers understand basic premises, have them latch onto basic concepts, so that they could enjoy the drama of each game from beginning to end, rather than just during the final two minutes when it was obvious someone had to score.

I think I finally knew we were heading in the right direction when Teddy Shaker, our executive producer, came up to me one day and said, "My wife watched the telecast yesterday and told me she's beginning to understand what pro basketball is all about."

That was the best thing anyone could have said to me, because that's what it was all about.

I held that job four years, and in each of those years the Celtics wound up making it into the finals, three times against the Lakers and once (1986) against the Rockets.

So each year I found myself on the receiving end of two escalating criticisms: Boston fans didn't think I was being fair to the Celtics, while fans and critics in opposing cities, especially LA and later Detroit, charged me with being a *homer*. It was simply too fine a line to walk without offending someone.

The Celtics and Lakers have been archrivals for almost thirty years, including the seasons I played—when, I suspect, some of these critics whacking me around today were probably kids watching me punch Rudy LaRusso in the chops. That one fistfight marked me forever as a villain in LA. Things like that used to go through my mind whenever I read a scorching review that bore no relation to the job I thought I did.

Anti-Celtics feeling is very real in the NBA. A few years ago a mutual friend arranged a get-together between Elgin Baylor and me. "You guys ought to get to know each other," he said. I had never spent any time with Elgin, but I always had tremendous respect for him. I still think he's the all-time forward; Larry Bird has yet to beat Elgin Baylor in *my* mind! So we shot the breeze for a few hours, and the next time I saw our friend he said, "You know, Elgin was very impressed by you." When I told him I didn't quite understand the relevance of that, he looked surprised: "Didn't you know? All those years you played with the Celtics he *hated* you!"

I was shocked. I had no idea.

But since then I've heard Billy Cunningham talk about how "arrogant" the Celtics are; I heard Jerry West, on an HBO special, pouring out anti-Celtics venom he's carried with him all these years; and everyone's heard Rick Barry bad-mouth Boston.

This bothers me, because these are people for whom I have enormous respect. I respected all those guys I played against—Johnny Kerr, Al Bianchi, Larry Costello, Dolph Schayes. *All of them!* Arrogant? What's arrogance? Sure, maybe Russell had what Carl Braun called "a kingly arrogance" about him, and Auerbach's "victory cigars" certainly didn't set well with some people, but there was never a championship series in which we weren't prepared to be gracious losers, in which we weren't prepared to walk into that other locker room and shake the hands of any team good enough to beat us. Okay, it happened only once in the nine years I played, but I know I was damn well prepared to do it every year.

The classic example of anti-Celtics sentiment occurred in 1971 when the league, celebrating its silver anniversary, asked a panel of "independent" writers to pick the finest team from those first twenty-five years. Did it pick the logical one, the one that captured eleven championships? No. It picked the 1966–67 Philadelphia 76ers, who won one title.

Give me a break! If that isn't the ultimate denial of

what happened, the ultimate withholding of approval, I don't know what is.

No matter how impartial I tried to be—and I tried very hard—there were bound to be people who could not accept me as objective, who could not disassociate that guy they saw in the booth from the one they saw in a Celtics uniform for nine years, then saw coaching the Celts for nine more.

The fact that I do color commentary on the Celtics' home games for SportsChannel didn't help, I'm sure.

I was doing Game 5 of the 1987 Boston-Detroit Eastern Conference finals for SportsChannel when Robert Parish belted Bill Laimbeer, really clobbered him, for which the league suspended him the following game. A tape of that telecast found its way to Detroit, where I was raked over the coals for not having *demanded* Parish's ejection. The fact is, I did point out that ejection was the normal penalty for such an attack. I guess people in Detroit were mad because I didn't stand up and scream for Parish's ouster. Because I had described his actions as "retaliation," they made it seem like I was endorsing what he did. My comment was, "Parish has had enough, so he threw a punch!" It was true. But I also attempted to explain that Laimbeer's style of play, because he's not a leaper, is to use his body, which a lot of players don't like.

I guess it didn't sell well in Detroit, but it was accurate.

That same series saw me branded a racist by Isiah Thomas, which I'll deal with more directly in the next chapter. He accused me and Billy Packer of perpetuating a stereotype that portrays white players as intelligent and black players as purely physical. It was a cheap shot, designed to get himself out of the hot water he was in for having racially denigrated Larry Bird, but it was an effective cheap shot: I got hate mail from all over the country for weeks after he leveled that accusation.

I don't know what that incident or the Parish incident or the ongoing charges of pro-Celtics bias might have had to do with it—I suspect all three were factors to some degree—but in the summer of 1987 the people at CBS decided to reassign me to a backup role on NBA telecasts, along with a similar role in the network's coverage of college basketball.

To this day, I don't know what prompted them to do that. Nobody's ever told me.

But at least I have the satisfaction of feeling good about what we did. It was a labor of love, and I think we succeeded in what we set out to accomplish, to turn the average NBA game into something analogous to an Ian Fleming novel, a story you don't want to put down—or, in our case, switch off—until it's over.

I'm an artist, okay? And the artist in me was gratified to have been a part of something that worked, to have been a contributor, along with other artists, in crafting something that was good enough to win record ratings, good enough to win an Emmy, something that made a valuable contribution to the popularity of a game that's been awfully good to me.

∘ 21 ∘

With Malice Toward None

Isiah Thomas ought to be grateful to Larry Bird for the rest of his life.

In fairness to him, it should be noted that he made his inflammatory remark after he had just seen his team lose a close Game 7 to the Celtics, 117–114, in the Eastern Conference finals of 1987. So he was tired and not sharp; and 530 press credentials had been issued for that series, which meant reporters were running all over the place looking for new angles, new slants.

But when Thomas suggested that Bird would be only an average player if he were black, that he was just the white man's superstar, he wasn't smiling. We had a CBS production meeting in which a tape of that remark was played. There are no erasers on live television. What you hear is what was said, and of the ten or twelve people attending that meeting who were trying to decide how CBS was going to handle this hot potato, opinion was pretty much split 50–50 as to whether Isiah really *meant* what he said.

When we convened in Los Angeles the following

weekend for the start of the Celtics–Lakers final, CBS flew Isiah there for a press conference at which Bird, appearing with him, stole the show while taking him off the hook: "I don't think Isiah is stupid. He knows I'm a *baaad* basketball player!" Everyone laughed, most of all Isiah. All Bird had to do to leave him twisting in the wind was to say nothing. Instead, he bailed him out; it was a beautiful thing for one ballplayer to do for another.

CBS then brought Isiah on at halftime of the next game to be Brent Musburger's special guest, allowing him yet another chance to wipe the slate clean by telling a national viewing audience it had all been an unfortunate misunderstanding.

That's quite a contrast to the way CBS handled Jimmy the Greek, who was made to look like Archie Bunker, six months later when they fired him.

In an off-the-cuff, unguarded interview, ironically on what would have been the fifty-ninth birthday of Dr. Martin Luther King, Jr., Jimmy tried explaining the reason for what he felt was the inherent superiority of black athletes over whites, suggesting blacks were "bred to be that way. . . . This goes back to the Civil War when, during the slave trading, the owner would breed his big black to his big woman so he could have a big black kid. See, this is where it all started."

I'm not an anthropologist, okay? I'm not endorsing what Jimmy said, or even trying to justify it, but I am questioning the manner in which he was treated compared to the treatment Isiah received.

They made Jimmy the Greek go away for saying that. The difference was that they *couldn't* make Isiah go away, even though it's my belief there was a hell of a lot more intentional malice in what Isiah said than there was in what Jimmy said.

Jimmy the Greek didn't miss seeing *Roots,* one of the greatest programs ever that gave white people insight into things black people had been talking about for years. *Roots* was not only superb theater; it was superb literature. I don't believe he's a racist. Why would Irv Cross, his black colleague at CBS, have stepped forward immediately in his defense, imperiling his own career and risking the alienation of his own people, if he and Jimmy hadn't shared some kind of meaningful relationship? My hat's off to Irv; he tried to do for Jimmy what Bird did for Isiah, but the difference was Jimmy never had a chance.

Jimmy had been around blacks too long and had dealt with too many of them on a social basis for too long to have harbored racist feelings without having them become known. That's why I had no trouble believing that he was either misunderstood, or what he attempted to say was not well-spoken.

It happens.

I was willing to believe that's what happened to Isiah when he took his shot at me. It was the day after he made his remark about Bird, before the press conference with Larry was scheduled, before he knew CBS would come to his rescue, and he was starting to get some heat. But instead of shutting up or looking for a way to defuse the issue, he went after me as a way of taking the spotlight off himself. He knew he had made a serious mistake, and his way of getting out of it was to try to make me the bad guy. That was as ironic as it was unfair, because while almost everyone else in the media was calling him dumb for blowing Game 5 by throwing a bad pass with five seconds to go, I tried giving him the benefit of the doubt on CBS, explaining how it could have happened. I pointed out how Bird, who picked off the pass, was partially hidden; and how Laimbeer, a *white* player, was equally at fault for backing up, rather than coming forward to receive the pass. I actually came to Isiah's defense when he was without a plea, and the next thing I knew he was practically calling me a redneck.

In essence, he said Billy Packer and I were guilty of perpetuating the stereotype that holds that blacks rely on physical skills while whites have a more intellectual approach to sports. In all the years I've worked for CBS I never received one letter of complaint along racial lines; all of a sudden, after Isiah's accusation, I got a ton of complaints. If his intention was to use me as a scapegoat to help get himself off the hook, he certainly succeeded.

I resented it, but I also understood it. Isiah was quite human in all of this. He proved that by telling Bird he was sorry, after which everyone was quick to forgive him. I was happy they did, because the mess he created could have been devastating to racial relations within the NBA.

But I'm still waiting for him to say he's sorry for what he did to me, too.

Racial relations are such a sensitive issue in this country, with radicals whipping up discord on both sides of the fence, that we're in danger of going on witch hunts. Someone seems to cast an aspersion at someone else, for whatever reason, and there's no presumption of innocence. *Guilty as charged!* Man, that's dangerous. If Isiah doesn't think he hurt me, personally as well as professionally, I'll be happy to show him my mail.

Jimmy the Greek, I believe, was the victim of a longstanding policy, shared by all the networks, that requires broadcasts to aim at advancing racial harmony.

It took hold in the 1960s, when cities were burning down, when people were marching, when people were dying—when, at times, a new Civil War seemed almost ready to erupt. There were commitments to justice made by a lot of people back then. The greatest thing John Fitzgerald Kennedy set out to do was to force America to experience what I had experienced on the Boston Celtics, to get Americans to tear down barriers and start working together for a common goal, a common good.

Networks made their commitments, too. Bill Cosby

did on TV what Sidney Poitier had been doing in films, showing blacks in human, sensitive situations, situations quite different from the Chattanooga Shoeshine Boy and Mr. Interlocutor on a Mississippi riverboat.

This was the networks' version of Affirmative Action, a concentrated effort to create a different image of black people in this country, showing them to be what they are: intelligent, talented, and as creative as anyone else. That was a statement that needed to be made, and the networks went out of their ways to make it. This was important, because the first thing a bigot must be made to realize is that these are ordinary people upon whom he's visiting all this hatred.

Now along came Jimmy the Greek, saying things that appeared to fly in the face of what everyone was trying to portray.

Irv Cross wasn't the only black who tried to save him.

Jesse Jackson rushed to his side, too, suggesting that perhaps instead of just preaching equality, the networks ought to start practicing it, too, by placing more minorities into positions of influence within their corporate hierarchies.

It made sense to me.

Ironically, Jimmy's inflammatory remark about blacks in positions of leadership ("The only things the whites control are the coaching jobs") was, even though he insists he said it tongue-in-cheek, an opportunity for basketball to feel good about itself. Six NBA championships have been won by black head coaches: Bill Russell (1968, 1969), Al Attles (1975), Lenny Wilkens (1979), and KC Jones (1984, 1986).

Generalities are always dangerous. So are labels, when you're applying them to people.

Nevertheless, the premise that holds that blacks play a more physical game while whites are more given to finesse is not without some merit, the wrath of militants notwithstanding.

There are no fundamentals in the schoolyard. It's whatever you can figure out for yourself, baby. If you don't get twelve baskets before the other side gets twelve baskets, you're off the court. It's that basic. So playground basketball becomes a jungle where the strong devour the weak. It's survival of the fittest. It's who can out-physical the other guy: Who can jump higher? Who can run faster? Who's stronger? It's an eight-year-old kid surveying the action and telling himself: *Hey, if I can't pick the ball off the backboard, I'm never gonna get a shot, not even in the warmups. So I'd better learn how to jump if I want to play.* That's where it starts. This is how the game is played. It's the way it was played in the schoolyards of Union City, where I first learned to give an elbow and take a shove.

It's *macho* ball. That's the way it's played in the cities. And who lives in the cities? More and more, urban populations are predominantly black. Basketball becomes more than just a recreation or a diversion for these kids. It becomes their statement. It's *who* they are! It's their identity, their credential, even their ticket out of the ghetto. There are thousands of kids who play basketball six hours a day, twelve months of the year, under some of the most adverse conditions you could imagine. On the playgrounds of Washington, New York, Philadelphia, Chicago, almost any big town, you can still hear people talking about the exploits of local legends who never left their neighborhoods, who never made it to college or the NBA, but who'll enjoy special status on those streets for the rest of their lives: "Hey, there goes a *basketball* player!"

A lot of great black players come out of that world.

It's not a world where everyone jumps into Mom's station wagon for a ride to the spic-and-span gym at St. Anne's Church where they'll have a two-hour

196

practice with nets and towels and showers, under the close supervision of five dads who've all read Adolph Rupp's book—"Okay guys, let's all line up. Now Johnny, you get on the outside and I'll pass it to you, then you can pass it over to Billy."

No one's doing 360-slam-dunks in St. Anne's Church. Players there are being taught the intricacies of setting picks, of working together in harmony, and they're learning it at a very young age in a very disciplined environment.

The kid who learns to *fly* in the schoolyard, who's enjoyed great success doing his own thing without much adult participation, may not be exposed to that kind of traditional coaching until he's almost ready for high school. He's picked up bad habits along the way, and now someone wants to change what he's been doing all his life. He's not only leery of that; he might even be resentful if he thinks he's being put down, because his game is what feeds his ego—he's proud of what he can do—and now someone's telling him that he's doing it all wrong. Hey, that's like attacking his manhood.

The point is, it's not a racist statement to say kids who come out of inner cities—and those are predominantly black kids—usually play a more physical brand of ball. It's not a statement born of any hatred or ill will; and what's more, it happens to be true.

I'm not inclined to wear credentials on my sleeve, but on this particular subject I confess to sensitivity because my feelings on these matters were well-established long before Isiah first dribbled a ball. I was living with, playing with, working with, and respecting guys who were fighting these battles way before young Mr. Thomas was even born.

There was the night in 1961, for example, when we gave the keys to his city back to the mayor of Marion, Indiana. We were on what was billed as a historic Southern trip, the highlight of which was going to be a game in Lexington, Kentucky, where, in honoring Frank Ramsey and Cliff Hagan, Rupp Arena would be opened to nonsegregated seating for the first time.

The Marion game had taken place the preceding night, following an afternoon luncheon at which the mayor gave each of us a ceremonial key. By the time the game ended there was only one diner open in town, and Carl Braun and I were already sitting in a back booth when we saw Sam Jones and Satch Sanders walk in, talk with the man at the counter, then walk back out. We heard the guy make some kind of comment about "not letting coloreds in here" just as a few more players arrived. We called them over, gathered up everyone's keys, then drove to the mayor's house, woke him up, and handed them back to him at two o'clock in the morning.

Cultural differences? We played basketball: *That* was our culture. Hell, KC Jones taught me how to dance. I was a good enough dancer, but KC was a great hoofer, so whenever we'd have a party coming up I'd say, "Hey, Case, give me a few moves, will you?" And he'd take me off to the side of a room and teach me all the latest steps, like Fred Astaire: *Heel one-two! Toe one-two!*

I could tell dozens of stories like that, little indications of the closeness we came to share, the feelings we came to have for one another. Color? You didn't even see color after a while.

I just wish this whole country could run the way those old Celtics teams ran. We were like a lab of human relations, proving over and over, to ourselves and to anyone else who was paying attention, that we could accomplish things beyond our wildest dreams if we just kept our focus on what we had in common rather than being concerned with whatever it was that might have made us different.

That's what those flags in Boston Garden are all about.

I love Satch Sanders.

KC Jones, Sam Jones, Willie Naulls—they are *friends*, people I care about as people, not just as former teammates, although the team is what brought us together.

Yet I never had a black teammate until Russell caught up with me our rookie year in Boston. I was the classic example of someone who comes from a white, ethnic neighborhood with all kinds of bugaboos about people he knows nothing about: *Never hit a black guy in the head! Always hit him in the stomach, or else you'll break your hand!* I used to hear that kind of stuff all the time.

Then I joined the Celtics and my enlightenment began. You never really get to know someone until you see him under pressure, until you see how he reacts when things get tough, how he bounces back. I watched black teammates excel under maximum pressure, and many's the game I thought to myself, "I hope I hold up as well as they do." That was the beginning of genuine respect, out of which came genuine affection, which then gave birth to a growing wish that I could tell everyone carrying a load of ignorance or hate: "Damn, I wish you could see and experience what I see and experience every day, and you'd never feel that way again."

I know there are people who do not like the NBA because its teams are predominantly black.

I was down at Hilton Head recently when some kids came up to me to talk about the game. One of them said, "Know why we like the Celtics? Because they've got the most white guys."

I said to him, "Hey, pal, you've got the wrong story. You just don't understand. . . ." And I tried explaining to them some of the things I had learned, having come from the same kind of background they did.

Don't misunderstand; I'm not saying I'm God's gift to the black race. But I've had the opportunity to see more, experience more, and learn more than a lot of people who are very vocal on the subject, including Isiah Thomas.

If you're a racist who wants to see white supremacy, it ain't gonna happen, okay? And if you're a racist whose only objective is Black Power, that ain't gonna happen, either. Or at least neither one of you is going to get your kicks from the NBA because basketball isn't played to establish racial superiority.

The NBA reminds me of a computer seminar I went to not long ago. I was thinking of becoming involved with this company, so I sat through a presentation even though I'm what they call computer illiterate; I know nothing about the field. But this head marketing guy, who's black, was explaining technical things in such a way that I was able to follow what he was saying and understand what it was the company was planning to do. That's an art form. And then the head finance guy takes over. He's Chinese and just as eloquent. Here were two guys with Master's and Ph.D. degrees up the kazoo, doing a magnificent job of walking a novice through a very complicated discussion; and yet out on the streets, I thought to myself, people who didn't know them probably dismissed them as dummies every day.

I could have sat there telling myself, "This is bullshit. He's black. What does he know?" But that would have been pretty dumb on my part; his skills were too obvious to deny.

Yet there are people who'll look at the NBA and deny the obvious skills of a basketball Ph.D., just because they have a problem with his color.

If you're one of those people who have trouble liking the NBA for that reason, all I can say is you're missing out on the best of what can be offered when it comes to the sport that's been my life. You're cheating yourself at your own enjoyment because you're limiting your appreciation of somebody else's greatness. Why? Because of his color? If you can't appreciate what someone is doing because of his color, then you're not just missing the best of what sports has to offer; you're missing the best of what life has to offer.

You have to be able to accept the fact that somebody of a different color, a different nationality, a different religion, *whatever* it is that's different, can be just as great as anyone else you happen to like; maybe even greater.

If you can't enjoy the NBA because you can't enjoy seeing blacks do well, which is what it comes down to for a lot of people, then I'm sorry for you. I really am.

The NBA is in the business of marketing basketball. It is not in the business of marketing race.

And if it ever permits its best players to be determined by bigots, white or black, then it will never be able to market them as what they really are, the best in the world at what they do.

° 22 °

A Matter of Style

People are always asking me what the "secret" of winning is, as if it's an old family recipe tucked away in a drawer.

It's no secret. By now it should be obvious.

The way to win, assuming you're starting out with an organization that's solid from the ownership on down, is to develop a team philosophy, just the way businesses develop company policies. *What are we trying to accomplish here? What are our goals? How do we intend to achieve them? What will be our game plan?*

Then you've got to find the right kind of people, people who can make that philosophy work. They may not be the most talented players in the league, but if they have drive and determination enough to accept the challenge you're proposing to them, and if they're then willing to blend their individual egos into one corporate ego that feeds them all, baby, now you've got a *team.*

And that's where it starts, when the ultimate consideration in every decision is, "What will be best for the team?"

The philosophy of the teams I played on and later coached was to attack the will of the other teams to beat us. I know, that sounds like something you hang over the locker room door, and everyone bows when he reads it; it's a great cliché. But we transformed that cliché into tactics and strategies that really did test our opponents, mentally and physically.

No one epitomizes team philosophy better today than Pat Riley's Lakers. He's the consummate coach when it comes to knowing how to utilize and milk out every advantage he has, how to enhance his "attack theory" at every opportunity—like putting James Worthy at the top of his defense, so that when LA goes the other way there's more apt to be a mismatch where a guard must pick up Worthy on a wing, leaving a forward to contend with Magic. There's a touch of genius in some of the things I see Riley do. He works speed as well as size into his mismatches. Worthy takes off twenty feet away from the basket and can run with any guard, so the guard who's stuck defending him either catches up to him in the air, which is a foul, or has to let him go by.

No team ever made the fast break work better than the Cousy-Russell teams I played on, but Riley's Lakers come the closest.

Any team that wins a championship has an impact on the pro game the following season.

Because the Lakers and Celtics have been so dominant in the 1980s, we're seeing their reflections in the way their conferences play. Right now the Western Conference is heavily into the fast break while the Eastern Conference, where the Celtics rely on a halfcourt game with multiple low-post options, is much more rock 'em and sock 'em. When you talk about teams like Atlanta and Detroit, you're talking about teams that can really bang! They don't go for that out west. It's almost getting to be like baseball with its American and National Leagues, where designated hitters and different strike zones give you two distinct versions of the same game.

Styles are so important that the Celtics went out and got Dennis Johnson a few years ago for the express purpose of stopping Philadelphia's Andrew Toney. That's pretty damn precise—it boils down to figuring you can win a title by the difference one matchup can make.

The Knickerbockers who won championships in 1970 and 1973 had an impact on the game that lasted five years.

That team was an aberration: Its big people were all great outside shooters and its little people were all good inside shooters. We always had a tough time beating them because whenever they missed a shot their big people were in perfect defensive position. My clubs were built on quickness, on beating the big guys down the court and wearing them out, but the big guys on the Knicks were already halfway there whenever a transition occurred.

Jerry Lucas, their center, loved tossing in long bombs the way Clyde Lovellette used to. The closest thing to Lucas and Lovellette right now is Bill Laimbeer, though he's a better rebounder than either of them was. Lucas was cute when it came to rebounds. At the end of every quarter he'd grab the ball so that the stat man would credit him with a rebound. There's a tabulating process going on all game long for the record books; for all those shots taken, there has to be a certain number of rebounds. If a guy takes a shot before the gun goes off, and he misses, they don't just throw that rebound away. There has to be an accounting for it. So Lucas used to run right over and grab the ball. I'll bet he got an extra three rebounds a game that way.

But those Knicks were best known for their defense. Steals came into vogue because Walt Frazier was stealing the ball in New York. The truth was, much of the credit for Frazier's steals should have gone to Dick Barnett. They played a gambling zone press that featured a lot of jump switches where you attack the ball on the dribble. Barnett usually did the hard part, taking the dribbler and pinning him to the sidelines, then making him spin, setting up the ball for the easy steal by Frazier. Everyone was saying, "Wow, look at Clyde go for the ball," when actually, all he had to do was time it right because the ball was already sitting there. The hard part of the job was the part Barnett did so well.

The zone press is a vulnerable defense, however. Once you beat the strength of it, the advantage swings to the offense, and the way to beat it is to attack the basket for layups. It becomes a question of how quickly you can get the ball upcourt and attack the basket. Then the defense has to rely on its shot-blocker. Hubie Brown's Knicks never had a shot-blocker, so Hubie imposed a no-layup rule that went like this: "No matter what, nobody gets a layup! You foul them first, make them shoot two free throws." Even that strategy had an impact on the game, because it led to a change in rules regarding deliberate fouls.

The other type of press is called a man-to-man, and it's much tougher to beat. If you beat one man, another man jumps up to take you, and they rotate. But generally everyone has a man, and the only way to beat it is to have a great ballhandler. You have everyone else run upcourt, then let the ballhandler figure a way to bring the ball to them.

When I coached the Celtics against Milwaukee in that 1974 championship series, we used a man-to-man on Oscar Robertson, forcing him to bring up the ball under maximum pressure, and we wore him out. In fact, the joke that made the rounds back then was that Oscar finally got into shape by the end of the series.

I loved the man-to-man. It was a great defense. It was like a 1930s boxing match, or maybe like Carmen Basilio and Sugar Ray Robinson in that 1958 blood-bath. Remember the picture: Basilio with the puffed-up eye and Robinson hardly able to stand? That was what the man-to-man was like.

Unfortunately, it pretty much fell by the wayside, for several reasons. The college coaches who began coming into the league didn't use it because the talent there wasn't as great. Then the league itself moved in with tough new rules, like the hand-checking rule aimed at curbing violence. The man-to-man is a very physical defense. And finally, with all the big con-tracts floating around, there weren't that many tough guys left to play it. That's why I would have wanted a Ronnie Lee on my team in Houston. The man-to-man required a special temperament, which became a van-ishing quality once financial security took much of the meanness out of the game.

The hook shot fell by the wayside, too, and why that happened is beyond me. It's as if there's a stigma attached to it, like it's a relic from the 1950s, which is ridiculous.

Every once in a while there are lessons from his-tory that get recycled, and I'm still waiting for the hook shot to be rediscovered. Whenever I see a kid like Brad Lohaus of the Celtics, I feel like pulling him aside and saying: "Look, all you have to do to get a good shot off, whenever you want to, is line up on the same side of the floor as your shooting hand [he happens to be a lefty], get into the low post, fake once with your head toward the middle, then turn toward the base line and let 'er rip, just like Abdul-Jabbar!"

But kids today won't do it.

Look at Kareem. What's he now, forty-one? That means thirty years ago when he was a kid, he watched those old-timers from the 1950s and emulated them, and look at how well that shot has served him all these years. So why aren't today's kids doing the same thing, emulating Kareem? It beats me. Here's a man who's scored more points than anyone else in the history of professional basketball, and I'll bet 95 percent of those points came on hook shots. Maybe they think he holds the patent on it.

I used to shoot the hook shot all the time. It's not only easier to shoot than a jumper; it's virtually impossible to defend, because your body is in the way of the defender, which means he can't block it unless he's significantly taller than you are or unless he's outfoxed you completely. And if he does try to outfox you, it requires such a dramatic gamble on his part that, unless you're a blithering idiot, all you have to do is tuck it in, take a dribble, and you'll have yourself a layup because he'll be way out of defensive position.

I don't care what era you're talking about, the hook shot works!

It was the high school coaches who attached the stigma to the hook, who stopped teaching it, who labeled it a "showoff" shot; and when they did that they did their kids a great disservice.

Coaches who limit their players' development in any way always do them a great disservice. One of my major beefs is with the high school coach who tells his big kids not to dribble the ball. The bigger the kid the less he wants to teach him how to dribble because he has the mistaken notion that anyone tall is going to have the ball stolen away.

In truth, what that coach is doing is undermining the kid's potential to become a real force out there. He's doing that by limiting his mobility, by limiting his chances to use his size advantage. Anyone who believes centers shouldn't dribble ought to take another look at Ralph Sampson or Akeem Olajuwon, because he obviously missed seeing Dave Cowens.

The coach who yells "Give the ball to the little guys" the minute the big guys touch it is missing an important point: *There is no defense that can shut you down if all five of your players know how to move the ball.* But moving the ball means being able to put it onto the floor, at least for a couple of dribbles.

Basketball is, above all, a game of mobility, and anyone who can't dribble is not a mobile player because he's locked into one spot.

Look at the way Kevin McHale increases his size advantage by being able to put the ball on the floor and *go* the moment he spots a weakness in the defense. It's not his size that drives opponents nuts; at 6'10", he doesn't scare anybody. What makes Kevin special is his mobility.

The high school coach who restricts a kid's mobility ought to realize that, in addition to cheating the player, he's also producing easy prey for the opposition.

If it's done unintentionally, it's a mistake.

If it's done on purpose, it's a shame.

It's my belief every player ought to be like a quarterback in football; that is, he should be able to read what the defense is doing, spot an opening, or anticipate where an opening is likely to appear.

Every great *pro* player should not only be able to read what the defense is doing, he should also know what it means to each of his teammates. Then the trick is to know which of those teammates now represents the best percentage play. *Four guys are open? If I have a choice, which one gets the ball?*

This is where the intelligence of the game comes in; this is what makes it a thinking man's game.

Larry Bird knows where every player is all the time, just the way Cousy used to know where to find all of us.

Or watch Kareem: He's the best big guy I ever saw at reading a defense and picking out the right open man for the best percentage shot. He never panics. He allows a play to develop, then passes beautifully.

What every coach should understand is that limited skills result in limited options.

The coach who works on developing all of his players' abilities, on developing all of the weapons in their arsenals, is really doing himself a favor, too, because he's broadening the base of his own strategies.

It makes no sense to handcuff yourself.

Now those arsenals have to include a good outside shot.

We have passed the apex of the Jump Shot Era, thanks in large measure to the introduction of the three-point basket, which, in my opinion, was the best thing to happen to pro basketball since the advent of the twenty-four-second clock.

The game had deteriorated to where the jump shot was everything, to where coaches in high school and college would scream like hell at any kid who took an outside shot. Outside shooting skills were as endangered as buffalos. I remember watching a championship high school game in Washington, D.C., and not seeing one kid on either side take a shot from farther than fifteen feet out, even in the warmups.

High school coaches and college coaches weren't teaching or encouraging outside shooting anymore. I could never understand that. If you don't have the outside "prove-it-to-us" shooters who can draw a defense out like an accordion, you're just inviting the other teams' big guys to pack it in around the basket.

This was finally driven home to a lot of people in the 1983 NCAA championship game when Jimmy Valvano's North Carolina State team, coming from the Atlantic Coast Conference, which pioneered the three-point shot in college ball, beat what everyone regarded as a superior Houston team by incorporating the three-point shot into its attack. Jimmy's kids simply shot right over Houston's great interior defense, which was anchored by Akeem Olajuwon, and everyone said, "Wow, what have we discovered here?"

But it was just another case of history recycling a valuable lesson that somehow had gotten lost along the way.

Go the NBA's All-Star weekend now and you'll find the biggest cheers are no longer reserved for the winner of the Slam-Dunk Contest. Sure, it was nice when Spud Webb won it, but the slam dunk has lost a lot of its luster.

Now fans cheer loudest for the Three-Point Shot winner, and kids all over the country, in learning how to shoot it, are going back to the basics of the push shot, which was *the* shot thirty years ago.

Watch Larry Bird, Magic Johnson, or Michael Cooper: They sort of take a jump shot, but what they're actually shooting, more and more, is a spruced-up version of the old Dolph Schayes push shot! That's always been a great shot, taken with ultimate ease; your body's behind it, so there's no pain, no strain.

The jump shot, conversely, is a difficult shot to shoot with precision over an entire game because your legs, which give it its distance, get tired. But when you release a push shot, it's almost like getting behind the ball and shot-putting it, drawing strength from your entire body, which gives you a lot more power than trying to flick it at the peak of a jump.

The three-point shot makes sense strategically, too.

Rick Pitino, who used it very effectively when he was coaching at Providence College, was the first one to point this out to me. A shooter who can make 33 percent of his three-point attempts is the equivalent to a shooter who makes 50 percent of his two-point tries. It's easy enough to demonstrate. Give each shooter 100 attempts. If the three-point shooter sinks one-third of his, he gets 99 points. The two-point shooter would have to sink 50 percent of his to match that.

So if you have a guy who can average 38, 40, or 42 percent from outside that three-point perimeter, he's more valuable to your team than the guy who stays inside and hits 50 percent, even though that's excellent shooting.

I often wonder what Ol' Dolph thinks whenever he looks at that stripe. I'll tell you what I think: If they'd had one on the floor of the Onondaga War Memorial in Syracuse, he'd have been good for 63 points a night.

Now strategies are changing again; or, to be more accurate, history's repeating itself again.

Coaches are once again on the lookout for players who can hit the outside shot. The threat of being able to make a three-pointer has not only added excitement to the game; it's also made two-pointers easier to take because the defense is caught in the middle. And what's more—what's even better—is that it's brought defensive speed back into the game; the guy now guarding the three-point shooter has to be quick enough to drop back five or six steps and help double-up on the big men when the ball is tossed inside.

What is it they say—the more things change, the more they stay the same?

So now pure shooters are back in style.

Forget Joltin' Joe. The pertinent question now, Mrs. Robinson, is: *Where have you gone, Downtown Freddy Brown?*

Wherever he is, I'm sure he's eating his heart out.

○ 23 ○

The Living Legends

The "living legends" of the NBA do, indeed, live on.

Don't forget, the NBA wasn't born until after World War II, so folks *can* remember, especially the era I played.

Just say *Wilt!* and basketball people know who you're talking about. The same with *Jerry!* or *Elgin!* or *Oscar!*

People remember them.

I'll remember them, too.

Jerry West was a great player in almost every aspect of the game. He was a great outside shooter and he was a great passer, which became evident in later years when he was asked to be the playmaker while Gail Goodrich played off-guard. And as anyone who ever matched up against him can tell you, he was a great defensive player.

He was also a freak, because he was so fast and had such a fantastic wing span. Certain players over the years have become great because no one's been able to play them—they *can't* play them because they're freaks. That was Jerry.

If you tried to match him against a man with similar speed, even a guy his own size, eyeball to eyeball, he'd just back him up with those long arms of his so that the guy couldn't even touch the ball, and then he'd go up for a jumper. If you tried to play a bigger man against him, to take away the jumper, he'd kill him with his speed; the bigger guy wouldn't be able to stay with him.

So there was no way to play Jerry West unless you had someone with arms as long and speed as fast, and there was no other creature like that in the league.

Elgin Baylor was the all-time great forward in my mind.

He had all the physical tools—passing, rebounding, shooting, plus he was a great leaper—but Elgin was also as smart as anyone who ever played the game. He knew his talents and he knew his teammates' talents, and he always seemed to know just the right way to use them all to their fullest advantage in every situation.

Baylor was the complete offensive package. That was widely known. Then, when Rudy LaRusso got hurt for a while, I made a startling discovery about Elgin: The sucker could play great defense, too.

LaRusso was one of the best defensive forwards around, but after tangling with Baylor once or twice, I found myself thinking, "Rudy, pal, come back! Please."

Oscar Robertson was the prototype of the big guard. He had magnificent passing skills, yet he couldn't beat you with speed and didn't dazzle you with footwork. In the current era of guards it would be hard to describe the Big O. He wasn't an outside shooter, but you wouldn't call him a point guard either, because he didn't have the hard push to force a tempo.

He had a style of his own, which Walt Frazier later duplicated; Frazier played exactly like Oscar. Robertson would back you down into the paint, into his range, play you one-on-one, then shoot over you— and if you tried to rush him or tried to help someone else cover him as he was making his move, he'd nail the open man with a perfect pass almost every time.

Wilt Chamberlain was listed as 7'1" 275 pounds, which I suspect were conservative estimates. He was also, in my judgment, the greatest athlete ever to play the game.

What Wilt did was take George Mikan's low-post ability and blow it out of sight. He was *the* physical player of all time. Nobody had an answer to him in a physical way, so teams began to beat the hell out of him. I would never have wanted to be Wilt Chamberlain. When I hear Kareem complaining about getting "manhandled," I smile; nobody was ever manhandled as much as Wilt. It was the tactic of every team in the league to grab him, to hold him, to whack him, because all it cost to do that was a foul; everyone knew he was a poor (51 percent) free-throw shooter. The fact they were able to get away with that all those years says a lot about Chamberlain's temperament. He rarely lost his cool or struck back. I give him a lot of credit for that. I'm sure it must have been irritating. But in addition to being basically a nice guy, he also understood that if he responded and got tossed out of a game, he'd have been playing right into the opposition's hands.

The only other way for him to have discouraged that treatment would have been to cash in on those trips to the free-throw line, but he never did. I think his strength worked against him. Wilt could stand almost at halfcourt, flatfooted, and make 20 out of 25 shots. I saw him do that. But when he'd get up to the foul line, within fifteen feet of the basket, he was so strong he couldn't soften his shot. The only time he had even modest success was when he stepped back to where his heels practically touched the top of the foul circle; then it became a soft shot for him.

The ultimate man-to-man battle of all time in the NBA was Russell versus Chamberlain. One was a physical giant and the other was a mental giant; it was mind over matter, brains against force, whenever they collided. You really had to understand the game to understand the level of excellence each of them brought to that battle. Since no one could beat Wilt physically, the answer was to outfox him, to outthink him, to outpsyche him, and this is where Russell left in his dust everyone else who ever played the game. I have never seen another player of Russell's mental stature at the center position, nor have I seen another player of Wilt's physical stature at the center position, which is why I don't think we'll ever see a confrontation as dramatic or classic as theirs again.

Russell and Chamberlain would out-rebound anybody in the NBA today, and it wouldn't be close. Those two put rebound records into the books—Wilt: 55 in one game, an average of 27 a game for a season; Russell: 51 in one game, an average of 24 a game for a season—that will never be touched, not the way the game is played now. People say, ''Oh, that's because you guys in the old days missed so many shots,'' which may be partially true. But that wasn't it. What made these two so special was their willingness to *go get the ball.*

There aren't very many guys in the NBA right now who are taught to do that, who are trained to do that, or who want to do that. Charles Barkley is one of them. Charles Barkley will *go get the ball.* Kareem Abdul-Jabbar will not *go get the ball.*

Then again, that's why Kareem has lasted all these years; he hasn't used up his legs and his back. Watch his socks. They stay up; they never lose their elasticity. That's because he plays the game on the floor. Kareem is a very competitive guy, but he never had that killer instinct for rebounds, which goes to show again that there's no such thing as a perfect basketball player.

Russell and Chamberlain fought their war on the ground, in the air, everywhere. Wilt once scored 100 points in a game. He once averaged 50.4 a game for an entire season. Russell never came close to scoring like that. Of course, he never tried. But he did win eleven championships in the thirteen years he played. Wilt won two, one of which came after Bill retired, and in both of those championship seasons he abandoned the big numbers and played the game the way Russell played it.

In fairness to Wilt, he was led and encouraged in the directions he went by coaches, writers, fans, even by his own PR.

I know it gnaws at him today whenever Russell's titles are thrown in his face. But in his own way Wilt was a big winner, too.

Russell certainly was, and still is, the loser when it comes to PR, and much of that is his own fault.

He could do the most boorish, rude things you'd ever imagine.

A group of us went to Rumania once to put on some clinics. We were having breakfast when this little grandmother came over to our table, said she was from Boston, and asked Russ for his autograph. He continued eating as she stood there. After an awkward moment, she pretended to believe he hadn't heard her, so she stepped closer and said, "Excuse me, Mr. Russell, but my grandson follows the Celtics and he would be thrilled if I could give him your autograph." Now she knew he had heard her. But he never looked up, never batted an eyelash; he wouldn't even explain his refusal, which at least would have allowed the lady to retreat with dignity. He gave her no way out. So this woman, well into her seventies, just stood there, totally embarrassed. Finally, I grabbed her book and passed it around to the rest of the guys, who couldn't wait to sign it. She thanked us, then quickly left.

That's an awful story; it's why Carl Braun would talk about Bill having a "kingly arrogance."

But there has to be a flip side. When an obviously intelligent man does something that atrocious, it's not rational, and it tells me this must be a hurtin' dude.

Russell had been hurt often, in many ways, and this is how it came out. I always thought of him as a latter-day Jack Johnson—the great black fighter who knew the white world hated him and said: "You've got to take me as I am. I'm *not* going to make it easy for you to like me."

That was Russell. He was like a tough little kid who's always making it extremely difficult to test whether you love him or not. That's what he was doing, even in his adult life.

He did not let people get to know him. He did not let people get close. He'd have been a great heavy-weight champion: He'd get knocked down, jump up, shake it off, and make believe you never laid a glove on him. That's the way he approached all of this stuff. There was a lot of bravado to him, yet under-neath it all was a very sensitive human being.

This is a man who once single-handedly won an All-Star Game—was flat-out the best player in it—yet didn't get the MVP trophy because a couple of writers from Boston didn't want to see it go to a black guy.

This is a man who had his suburban Boston home broken into more than once, who returned—probably after hearing Garden crowds cheer him for the glory he brought to their city—to find his trophies smashed, to find racial epithets left behind by robbers who'd defecated in his bed.

This is a man who broke down and cried when the people of the suburban town he lived in as a rookie had a dinner to show their appreciation of him—the same town where he later found he was unable to purchase a house.

There are so many things that happened over the years to hurt this guy, things most people still don't know about because he's too proud to mention them. If Russell identified particular incidents, no matter how outrageous they were, he'd be admitting to the people who perpetrated them that they had been suc-cessful in hurting him, and there was no damn way in the world he was ever going to admit that. So, to this day, he never gets into specifics; he just says he doesn't like Boston, and people in Boston get offended. If they knew the whole story, they'd understand it better.

Those of us who watched it happen understand why Russell feels the way he does today.

Sometimes he doesn't make it easy for us to like him, either.

But if I had to pick one guy to have on my side for any fight I was facing, Russell would be the guy, because he would do whatever he felt had to be done to win. He'd think about it, then he'd execute it with the fiercest drive for victory I've ever seen.

Bill Russell was the all-time winner.

I tell kids today, "Oh, I wish you could have seen Bob Cousy pass the ball and run the fast break!"

He was the Michelangelo of basketball.

Magic Johnson? He might be its Picasso.

Picasso built upon the things he learned from Michelangelo—that was Cooz.

Cooz was the guy who put it all down on paper, who first showed how it could be done, who laid out all the basics for the famous artists who followed, and who did so with a creative flair that's never been equaled, let alone surpassed.

He's still *Mister Basketball* to me.

Dave DeBusschere, until Larry Bird came along, was the last of the old-time forwards. That's why I call Bird the prehistoric forward; it's as if Auerbach found him in a cave somewhere, encased in a block of ice, and chipped him free. He plays the game a lot like Dave DeBusschere did.

Dave had all the skills: He could pass, rebound, shoot the ball, play defense. There are very few forwards who can do all that. Bird obviously can. And James Worthy is beginning to extend his range, to take it to the hoop more, to play a little better defense.

But there are very few guys like DeBusschere around today.

There were a lot before him, like Bob Pettit, the prototype of the power forward, who could play outside and still be a dominant rebounder.

There have not been very many since.

And then there was Doctor J.

Julius Erving brought to the game what Cousy brought to the game: great showmanship. And, like Cooz, he did it at a time when the game really needed it.

The Doctor was a competitor who did fantastic things with the ball—though I thought Elgin was a better passer—and he was the one who sort of crystallized the era of the dunk. But it wasn't just *how* he dunked, as spectacular as that was; it was *when* he dunked!

There was a lot of the Cooz in Doctor J when it came to picking the psychologically correct moment to make the play that would ignite his team, that would totally demoralize the opposition. It became a macho thing for the 76ers—their identity play—to see Doc soar in for a magnificent slam on the front end of a fast break.

A play like that could be good for as many as 10 points. You had to call a timeout almost every time Doc did it, because it got his team so hepped up you were in danger of being drowned by a tidal wave of emotion.

When a player can devastate the opposition on the basis of style alone, you'd better believe he belongs up there with the all-time greats.

There were many more outstanding players I'll remember with great affection and great admiration.

But let me play with these—Jerry; Elgin; Oscar; Wilt; Russell; Cooz; DeBusschere; Pettit; Doc; with Auerbach as our coach—and I'll take my chances, because I don't think there's a team in the world that could ever beat us.

∘ **24** ∘

The Now Generation

The NBA I joined had eight teams, ten players per roster.

Today's NBA has grown to twenty-five teams.

That means there will be 170 players who wouldn't even be in the league if the pro basketball market was still as tight as the one that existed in 1956.

The numbers make a convincing case that the game's been watered down, that it's easier to become a pro today.

Maybe so. But in many ways I think it's harder to be a good pro today, at least on a consistent basis.

The big money has not only done a lot to erode incentive, which translates into motivation, but it has also created potential morale problems. You're fighting to get that million-dollar contract because the player dressing next to you just got his; or maybe you feel your place in the financial pecking order no longer reflects your value to the team because a newcomer signed a deal that threw the whole picture out of whack.

We didn't have those problems, certainly not to the extent today's players do. Our sole reason for playing the game was that we enjoyed it. We were basketball bums. There wasn't enough money at stake to wreck friendships or to poison team spirit. We weren't inclined to peek inside each other's wallets.

I sometimes wonder if today's players get the same enjoyment from the game that we did, the same kick, the same gratification. Clearly Bird does; Magic does. And look at Kareem whenever he wins: Man, he *loves* it.

But overall, I've always suspected we enjoyed it more.

Part of the reason might be we didn't play as many games.

Much has been made of the fact NBA champions have difficulty repeating. I don't see any mystery to it. When we won our first championship in Game 7 against St. Louis, the date was April 13. Now championships aren't won until mid-June, which means there's less time to make the emotional turnaround, to come back healed and refreshed for what's going to be an even stiffer challenge the second time around, when everyone in the league is waiting to gun you down.

It's not as easy as it looks. It never has been.

The great ones just make it seem that way.

They did in my day, and they still do today.

Kareem Abdul-Jabbar is one of them. What you're seeing when you look at him is the culmination of nineteen years of dedication. He's not only a dominant player in terms of his scoring, but he's also become a very effective creator of offense for his teammates. Because outside shooting almost disappeared from the game for a long while, defenses got used to sagging, to clogging the areas near the basket, and Kareem found himself being double- and even triple-teamed. His sky hook had become an automatic two points in any halfcourt game, so "Stop Kareem" defenses were devised throughout the league.

His answer to that challenge was a real measure of his greatness. He had to develop another skill, another approach to the game that was much more intellectual than physical. And he did it. He became the best big man I ever saw at picking apart a defense with a perfect pass to an open teammate.

It was like a tackle learning how to become a quarterback; that's what this guy did. Watch the way he'll use a cutter as a decoy.

He's mastered all the little tricks of ball movement, of opening up a game; tricks that come through experience, observation, and dedication.

No big man has ever done it better.

Akeem Olajuwon is coming on fast, though.

He's got all the moves he needs for one-on-one; his next task is finding out how to solve the "Stop Akeem" defenses, which means he has to steal a page from Abdul-Jabbar's book.

He's facng the same situations Kareem did, but he hasn't got all the variables down the way Kareem has; Kareem's like a computer out there now. When the strength of a defense is put against Olajuwon, he's got to know it means an opening's been created somewhere else on the floor. That's his next challenge, to pick out those weaknesses and exploit them, but he hasn't got the poise or passing skills to do that yet. I don't think he's got the confidence either, but it's coming. Bill Fitch is doing a super job of bringing him along. He's already one of the fastest centers to ever play the game, and he has fantastic stamina. He even has a bit of Moses Malone in him in the way he seems to play better in the fourth quarter.

He's not Kareem yet. But he's looking more like his heir apparent all the time.

Larry Bird and Magic Johnson are the Chamberlain versus Russell of today—although, because they play different positions, they never really face each other. Still, like Chamberlain and Russell, they're two historic players, two fierce egos pushing each other harder and harder, bringing out the best in each other while bringing out the best in themselves.

Bird, to me, is the Bobby Fischer of basketball.

He's playing chess out there while everybody else is playing checkers. He's five moves ahead of the rest of the field in anticipating what people are going to do, and that's the fun of basketball for him. To other players, the fun might be how high they can jump: *I'm going to stuff this next one in backwards!* And that becomes their big challenge.

With Bird the challenge is all in the mind. He's a throwback to the old days; a thinking player.

That's what's made Magic come on so strong in recent years: He's become a smart player, too. His decisions on when and where to pass the ball are almost flawless now.

You've got to realize, these are two 6'9" guys who are slow. But, man, how they use their heads.

I think what people respect most about Bird is that he projects an old-fashioned work ethic. He's not doing it with celebrity and flash, because he doesn't have great athletic ability. What you're seeing in him is tenacity. That's his game. He's the blue-collar superstar.

Magic's becoming a lot like Oscar, playing the fast-break middle position the way Oscar used to, hitting open men on the fly rather than hard-pushing the ball upcourt himself. He tries to hard-push whenever he can, but he really can't beat many people down the floor, so he relies more on the natural advantage he has in being bigger than most of the people he faces. All he's got to do is keep the ball away from the man guarding him, then look over the defense until he spots an open teammate, usually for an easy layup.

Michael Cooper, Magic's Lakers teammate, is another player for whom I have the utmost respect. When I looked for players as a coach I looked for some hint, some indication of interior motivation, some trace of a drive that would already be there, that wouldn't require the urging of a coach.

That's Michael Cooper all over.

He's improved every single year, even though he's

been asked to play three different positions. He came up as a forward; now he's the backup for Magic, their point guard when Magic isn't in there, and he's also a defensive specialist when they put him in as the off-guard. He's just a dynamite all-around player: passer, rebounder, outside shooter—my kind of guy. And best of all, he's a nails player, baby. He's *in your jersey* all night and will kill to win.

Charles Barkley is like that. I like Charles Barkley.

So is Kevin McHale, to a degree. Kevin McHale is Bob Pettit all over again, only Pettit could go out twenty feet and still beat you. He was a forward, and in those days the pivot belonged to the center, but whenever Pettit went into the low post he played it just the way McHale does.

McHale's a bit of a freak, too. With those long arms he's able to create a lot of mismatches. There are very few people who can stop him one-on-one, and it's only for a game or two, if they're lucky. He's pretty cute when it comes to figuring out what a guy did to stop him the last time and then finding new ways to give him trouble the next time they meet. He's especially good at finding a soft spot in the defense and barreling right through it. Yet he still has the passing ability to create opportunities for his teammates, so you're never quite sure how to guard him. If you double him, he'll burn you with passes. If you back off, he'll burn you with his fakes and his shot. He really plays a head game with opponents.

I get that same feeling of déjà vu watching a kid like Brad Sellers. He's Bob McAdoo all over again—or could be.

I always thought McAdoo's correct position would have been quick forward. He had the speed to play defense like a 6'6" guy, yet at 6'9" he could run you into the pivot. No matter what you tried to do to stop him, McAdoo could hurt you. He burned big guys from the outside and little guys from the inside. Unfortunately, in his peak years at Buffalo they had to use him as a center. When the Lakers finally put him at forward he was a great help to them, but that was at the tail end of his career. In fact, one of the reasons the Lakers lost the 1984 finals to the Celtics was that McAdoo was hurt—a little-reported fact in Boston.

Sellers, a seven-footer, has all of McAdoo's possibilities. He shoots very well from outside and is just learning how to use his speed as a forward after half-running his way through Ohio State as a center.

Doug Collins, his coach at Chicago, is doing a smart thing in getting him adjusted to the rhythms of forward. He doesn't have the bulk to make an effective center anyway, so if they can capitalize on his speed he's going to be quite a problem. If smaller guys try to take him on, it'll be layupsville. And if big guys try to stop him, he'll just scorch them from outside.

Right now I'd call him a potential freak.

At the other end of the height chart there are three guys causing a lot of people to go back to the drawing boards: Tyrone Bogues, 5'3"; Spud Webb, 5'7"; and Michael Adams, 5'9".

They make their size irrelevant with their speed.

The court is ninety-four feet long, and size is important only when you're within ten feet of the basket. That means speed is the prerequisite for the rest of that footage. Everyone's marveling at what these guys are doing. Defenders, fearful of being beaten, are backpedaling like defensive backs wary of wide receivers. They're so far off that size means nothing.

But this is not a new phenomenon; it's just another one of those lessons from history that gets recycled every so often. Calvin Murphy, who was 5'9", first demonstrated it to me as I watched him drive on Jo Jo White. Jo Jo had decent speed, but when he saw Calvin coming at him with all burners going, he went into such a retreat that he was still moving backward when Calvin stopped to pop. The shot was his, wide open. He had intimidated the defense into giving it to him.

A couple of years ago I was talking with Dean Smith, the North Carolina coach, telling him what a great weapon this kid Webb was, how the fastest players in the league wanted no part of guarding him.

"You think he's good?" Dean said. "Wait'll you see Mugsy Bogues. He's the only player, in all my years of coaching, who ever made me change my defense."

That's some compliment.

The point is, speed will always have its place in this game. There just aren't enough Pat Rileys and Doug Moes to keep driving that message home.

That's why I like what Spud, Tyrone, and Michael represent.

That's my kind of basketball they're playing.

Isiah Thomas has the potential to become one of the all-time greats, but in order for that to happen he first has to become the consummate no-mistake passer and learn to read defenses all the time. He still takes things on by himself too much. And yet I've seen him in All-Star situations where he blew away the opposition by creating so many opportunities for his teammates that by game's end the defense didn't have a clue as to how to play him.

There's no question about his ability to play superstar ball. The question with Isiah is, why doesn't he play that way all the time? And he's the only one who can answer it.

Michael Jordan and Dominique Wilkins are both on the threshold of a special kind of stardom.

Michael is already one of the all-time great physical players, and Dominique is totally capable of demoralizing a team all by himself. There's just one more plateau they've both got to scale, and that's to add complete finesse to their incomparable physical skills.

Dominique is strong, a high-flier, and he's expanded his game to where he now can hit that outside shot. But he still doesn't read game situations, which is the ultimate finesse: *When do I pass? When do I shoot? When will it have the most impact if I score?* It's knowing how to pick your spots.

Michael's in the same boat. He's dominated people physically to this point. When he takes off, his glide path to the basket can leave three guys in its wake. He'll fly by one guy, stay up as he passes the second, who's trying to block his shot, and still go by a third defender. His gifts are remarkable.

But both of these guys have a tendency to force the play, to always be thinking that *now* is the time to take the shot, rather than keeping the defenses guessing. They have the ability to outfox defenses, but they don't use it nearly enough.

The great player does a number on the defense. If he takes it to the hoop and they jam him, he reads that and passes off, creating an easy opening for someone else on his team. He makes his teammates look good. Now if the other team starts playing him to make the pass the next time he comes down the court, then he's got to take the shot. The great player, the finesse player, works the defense to his advantage, saving those scoring situations for when they'll mean the most. He'll have the defense looking for the pass, backing off and backing off some more, until ultimately it's opened up a path for him to get an easy two points on the last play of the game.

When Dominique gets the ball at the end of a game now, everyone knows he's going for the shot, that he's not going to pass. So the defense uses that against him. There's no mystery to him. He's not trying to outthink the opposition. He's just trying to overwhelm them. He's forfeiting the element of surprise, which is a big mistake because that can win you a lot of ball games.

Michael's doing the same thing. Right now he can

score 63 points and lose a ball game. That's not good enough.

One of the things he's still in the process of learning is how to make everyone else on his team a better player. What would make him truly great, in my opinion, would be if he held back 75 percent of the time, using himself as a decoy and making it easier for teammates with less talent to score, saving himself for those true Michael Jordan moves when they're needed most.

He's got to become the base, the foundation, of his team's entire offense, the guy who'll get them two when two are needed, the way Bird does for the Celtics. He's got to become the go-to guy whom nobody can stop when the game is on the line. Right now all of his energies are expended in getting a ton of points when he should be saving some of those unique abilities for situations where nobody else can deliver.

Most players see only the one-on-one battle in front of them. They don't see other things happening that may be relevant to what they're doing.

The essence of finesse is to see the whole game around you while you're going through it. That's what Bird does and what Magic does. That's what makes them so special.

And that's what Michael and Dominique have to do next.

It's putting together the geometry of the game, which, to me, was always the most fun. It was the part of the game Russell and Cousy loved—the mind games, the psychology, the ability to almost will yourself to victory by destroying the will of the other guy to beat you. At times that feeling was so strong, so unmistakable, so real, that it was almost like looking at the other team and delivering a win by mental telepathy. It was a look you had in your eye, a message you wanted to deliver; and when the other team saw that look, it knew what it meant, it knew what was coming, and it wanted no part of it.

That happens when you get a whole team functioning as one. It doesn't happen when you have a superstar and four supporting actors.

What Michael Jordan wants to do now, I think, is take that next step. So does Dominique. All you have to do is watch them to understand what great competitors they are; baby, these guys want to win!

But pure physical talents aren't going to do it.

When a Jordan or a Wilkins makes all of his teammates potential scoring threats, too, it gets the opposition thinking, "Damn, how are we going to beat them *all?*" And it then allows them to become ultimate creators, the choreographers who decide how the game will be won.

Man, *that* is the stuff of superstars. Not many can do it.

These two can, if they decide to.

The beauty of basketball is that new stars keep coming along, just when you think you've seen everything.

Even now, somewhere on a playground, somewhere in a gym, there's a young Michael, a young Oscar, putting together all the skills that will have the NBA knocking on his door some day.

Maybe you can spot him. Don't look for the spectacular moves; they probably haven't blossomed yet. Just look for a fire in the eyes, or what Pat Riley likes to call "tough-mindedness."

It's almost that easy to spot.

Every time I see it I want to say, "Way to go, kid. Keep it up. As long as that fire keeps burning, who knows . . . ?"

○ 25 ○
A Losing Trip

Athletes have always faced temptations. That's nothing new. There's always been *something* that could distract them enough to keep them from getting where they wanted to go, whether it was booze, women, or horses.

But the big one they're facing now, drugs, is different from the others in one significant respect: This one can kill them without warning.

So why do they start? Why did Len Bias start?

I suspect there are several reasons.

Certainly there's peer pressure. Drugs are an accepted medium of social intercourse now. If you don't do them, you're not with it. Or so kids are told. You're looked at somewhat askance—you're a freak—and there aren't many kids walking around in the modern world who are willing to be individuals. So this becomes a matter of identity. I'm sure Len Bias, with all the fame and fortune he was about to enjoy as the first-round pick of the Boston Celtics, still wanted very much to be looked upon by his friends as just one of the guys.

I think drugs also serve as a common denominator for people who have an acceptance problem, particularly between the sexes. The social intercourse that leads to sexual intercourse is enhanced by the currency of drugs; to have drugs is to have something to offer in lieu of yourself, if you're not a sufficiently self-confident person.

Then there are people who tell me drugs are recreational. That's the one explanation I've never understood. What's recreational about them? What's the definition of recreation? Isn't it supposed to be the refreshing of the mind and the body, the restoring of spent energies? How does anesthetizing yourself fit into that? If your way of relaxing is to get away from who you really are, to escape your own personhood, you've got a serious problem.

And then there are those people who are truly hooked for psychological reasons, who are hurting in a variety of ways, most of which involve deprivation of love or self-esteem, who look to drugs as a way to dull these emotions, to make them go away: *If I don't feel them, they won't hurt.*

I didn't give a lot of thought to the drug culture until the last two years I coached. That's when marijuana and cocaine were beginning to surface as widespread problems in the league. I suspect they were problems long before I was aware of them, but that's when coaches first began talking about them in terms of how you could recognize signs that some of your players might be in trouble. I remember thinking then that one of the things I hated about this stuff was the paranoia it invited.

If you ask me whether I can tell if a player is on drugs, I've got to tell you I'm not sure.

Dick Stockton and I did a telecast for CBS in which we voted Quintin Dailey the star of the game after Chicago beat the Houston Rockets. Three days later, Dailey checked into a rehab clinic.

So if you ask me whether drugs hurt performance, I suppose I'd have to tell you I'm not sure about that either, though my guess is yes, because, if nothing else, they make those performances erratic, and a real professional is someone who gives you the same effort, the same game, the same dedication every night. That's my definition of a pro's pro. That was Havlicek, that was Baylor, that was West—night after night, the production never varied. The world could be blowing up and they'd still have their minds focused like laser beams on winning.

That's one thing drugs take away, I think: the focusing.

Walter Davis always struck me as having the professional discipline of a Larry Bird or a Magic Johnson, so when I heard he had a drug problem I was shocked.

He was a competitor, fiercely so. He played hard all the time, and on top of that everything I was ever told about him just reaffirmed my own opinion that this was the consummate pro, an intelligent guy who had it all together.

Then this stuff grabbed him.

After the first time comes the *second* time. I watched Walter one night on ESPN with Roy Firestone, and as they talked I thought to myself, "This damn stuff not only ruins people, it turns them into liars. Junkies lie. They lie to the public, but the real tragedy is they also lie to themselves."

The lie is telling themselves it doesn't matter. That's the ultimate lie, because it does matter. If it can make a Walter Davis believe it poses no threat to his career, then it's got to be a damn deceiving substance. Watching him that night bothered the hell out of me. It made me realize this could happen to anybody, yet if someone tried to tell me Bird or Magic had the same problem, I'd have to see it for myself before I'd believe it. I just can't imagine either one of those two giving away even a half-inch advantage; they've worked too hard to get those half-inch advantages.

Then again, I wouldn't have believed it of Walter Davis either.

Bill Fitch said something I took to heart when two of his players—Mitchell Wiggins and Lewis Lloyd— were suspended for drug usage. "Their *wives* didn't know," he said, "and they're a lot closer to these guys than I am. People knock us [the NBA] for our drug problem, believing it all starts with the money these guys make, but that's not where it begins. By the time a lot of these kids get to us they've already got a problem that started back in college."

I think he's right. Len Bias certainly was an example of that.

Lennie was an example of something else, too.

I'm no expert on any of this stuff. Maybe you *can* use it "recreationally" for an indefinite period. But, baby, it still has the propensity to jump up and kill you the next time!

It's Russian Roulette. That's all it is.

And no matter how lucky you think you are, if you play Russian Roulette long enough, you're going to lose.

Michael Ray Richardson had the potential to be another Magic Johnson, truly a great basketball star, if only he could have controlled this stuff.

His New Jersey teammates had compassion for him the first time, but the second time around really frustrated them. I know; they told me. He was going to be the leader of that club, the guy they were going to need to win all of those games, the one who was going to help them achieve all of their ambitions. He was just about to deliver that kind of leadership when his drug addiction chased him out of the league.

The leader was gone, and he'd taken the group's dream with him. Resentful? Of course they were.

I don't know what the answer is. I'm not even sure what all of this says—except I know what it says to me.

The ultimate high is to enjoy what you do with your emotions unencumbered. It's walking out of a basketball game after having focused all that you are—your intellect, your passions, your body—on a specific goal, and then seeing the desired result. It worked! *You worked!* That is the ultimate high, a high that can't be duplicated with a substance. What more is there than knowing that you maximized what you are? But to maximize what you are has to be done without additives, because the additives aren't you. When you need an additive to produce that high, the high you're getting is a deception. You think you're producing it when really it's the product of the substance. It's not a natural high. It's a synthetic high. How can that possibly be as good?

If you're going to maximize yourself, then you have to be willing to accept the fact you can fail. That's a very important part of appreciating success. If you just win-win-win all the time, with each succeeding win you find you appreciate it less. You have to drop down once in a while and experience some pain in order to understand the good feeling of victory. If people can't accept the fact they might fail, they can't ever fully appreciate victory; and they certainly won't experience the ultimate high that personal victories bring.

I'm not a masochist. Yet the artist in me knows I'm color-blind if I don't experience pain in my life. I'll become a robot. I won't see the full range of colors life has to offer if my emotions are distilled.

I'm afraid this is what's happening all around us. We're raising a whole generation of people who, for whatever reason, can't stand losing. Instead of allowing themselves to experience a full scale of emotions, young people choose to believe the world owes them a constant high.

That's what drugs are: They're instant *feel good,* made readily available by devious, unscrupulous suppliers; and who doesn't want to feel good?

Who doesn't want to feel like a winner?

The cruel irony is, it's their slavery to this stuff that's turning kids into genuine losers.

They're opting for a "Don't bother me" existence.

But how can there be any gratification in the avoidance of something?

You're not having a vital life if you're not making decisions, accepting challenges, taking the risk of losing big in order to know what it's like to win big. You can't be so afraid of failing that you don't try to accomplish anything.

Yet I've known people who were as afraid of being the hero as they were of being the goat. They couldn't deal with success any more than they could deal with failure; they just wanted to pass through life without making waves.

Hell, nobody gets through life without experiencing some kind of frustration. Ted Williams still talks about the pitchers he *couldn't* hit, and that sucker was the best hitter who ever lived! That's what it's all about— the old Kipling bit on meeting Triumph and Disaster and treating them both the same, learning to live and deal with both of them.

The lie of drugs is that none of this matters, so why not drop out? Why not take a pass? Why not skip the aggravation?

I have a hard time identifying with that, because I've never wanted to alter my state; I've gotten too much gratification from the realities in my life. I have an appreciation of highs and lows and of what place they have in the spectrum of my emotions.

But I do know this: It's only when you admit you're a loser and then experience the psychological pain of realizing you don't want to be a loser anymore, that the process of bouncing back begins, starting with the biggest step of all—walking away from the lie and getting on with what's left of your life.

It's not easy. But it can be done. And, man, it's sure worth the effort.

° **26** °

On the Road Again

Nothing threatens a pro sports marriage more than the day Hubby comes home for good.

No more training camps. No more road trips. No more escape.

It's what I call the Chinese water torture—the drip, drip, drip of everyday routine, of two people who now sit down together at breakfast every morning to deal with each other in a way they never have before.

What they find out, in many instances, is that they don't even know each other.

The first two years of marriage, in my opinion, are the most important. That's when the big adjustments have to be made. That's when most of the friction occurs. It's friction that's necessary, friction that's important, like the friction that polishes a diamond; and what makes it bearable is that there's all of this love and infatuation to get the two partners through it, to provide a glue, slowly cementing the relationship.

Years later, when they've both settled into being who they really are, that same friction might be very difficult to endure. The newness is gone and there's no more glue for recementing.

That's why it's dangerous if those first two years are constantly interrupted by periods of prolonged separation, periods when there's no communication, when that friction has to be postponed.

Yet this is exactly what happens in every pro sports marriage. Husbands and wives aren't together all the time, aren't growing as a couple, and when they are together they're always making accommodations for their unconventional life-style, further postponing the friction that inevitably must take place. He comes back from a trip and says, "Let's go out to eat," figuring she's been in the house all this time, though he really doesn't feel like going out at all. Or she keeps the house quiet all morning so he can sleep. Confrontations are avoided whenever possible.

The husband, meanwhile, is becoming increasingly assertive in his pursuit of athletic success—*and* increasingly egocentric, because that's the nature of his business. The wife, if she's to avoid a sense of having been left behind, has to be able to deal with his expanding world, to participate in it, to not feel threatened by it, to not feel threatened by *him*, and that takes a pretty special gal if she's only twenty-two.

I remember sitting down with my son one evening, not long after he got married. Both he and my daughter-in-law are very highly motivated, individualistic people, so they were getting into a lot of arguments at the time, including a couple in which it sounded as if they were going to kill each other.

"You know," I said to him, "some people might tell you two that it's wrong to be arguing this much. But I'm going to tell you that *they* are wrong. The beautiful thing is that you're both such strong personalities. You wouldn't be arguing if you didn't feel you had something to offer each other. So the arguments are not what's important. What's important is how you resolve them. When one of you gives in, that person shouldn't feel like a martyr or become resentful, nor should the other person feel like a victor. It's great to have strong feelings, great to state your cases, but just make sure both of you understand that whoever winds up conceding is conceding out of love. That way no one loses. You both win."

The gal who marries a professional athlete has to be able to maintain her own sense of worth while living with someone who's idolized by strangers. That's not easy.

Many wives have forfeited their thoughts, their opinions, their whole personalities because they couldn't compete with their husbands' popularity.

Others have grown resentful of the fact that no one even notices their merits. They're just "Mrs. So-and-so."

On top of everything else, they also have to deal with the fact that when their husbands are out on the road it means they're out in the world, a world of temptations.

Pro sports aren't unique when it comes to boys and girls. Many a marriage has crashed on the rocks of an office romance, and wives of traveling salesmen have to cope with insecurities, too.

But traveling salesmen, as a rule, aren't fantasy figures.

Athletes are.

There's erotica in basketball.

First of all, basketball players are better athletes and, as a rule, better looking than guys who play other sports. A basketball player in lousy shape is in better shape than a baseball player in great shape.

He's also running around more exposed than any other athlete, playing a sport where bodies glisten and strain and rub against each other, all of which is taking place in very close proximity to the customers.

Women fantasize, just the way men do, though

239

husbands don't want to believe that. Have you ever seen a film clip of women going "Whoop-dee-do!" at a male strip club? It's a catharsis; it allows them to come out of themselves for a while. Well, what did those ladies do before male strippers came along? Where did they bring those feelings, those urges? To the beach, to see a couple of guys prancing back and forth, if they were lucky?

No. They went to a basketball game.

When I was playing ball I'd take insurance clients—paunchy business types—out to dinner, and while they were talking about the game their wives would quietly ask me what Willie Naulls was like. Sure, their interest was masked so that nobody could really take offense, but there was no doubt in the world that what they were really getting at was "Do you know anything about him in the rack?"

Understand, Willie didn't play that much; he was on the bench most of the time, backing me up. So since there was no reason for them to zero in on the basketball ability of someone they hadn't seen in action, it was rather obvious they were attracted to Willie by something other than his jump shot.

I ran into that all the time.

When I was coaching I heard a woman turn to the gal next to her and say, "I'd love to take Jo Jo White to bed—as long as he didn't talk!"

It was that direct. All she wanted was his body.

Opportunities for amorous adventures were plentiful, and each guy handled them in his own way, according to whatever was relevant to him and his life.

Some had tremendous sexual appetites and chased any skirt they saw, trying to prove to themselves that they could have every woman in the world from A to Z.

Others abstained totally, remaining true to their

wives. Then there were guys who went through several stages. Everyone understood what was going on, and players who personally may have disapproved of certain situations nevertheless tried to be tolerant of others on the team who didn't share their views. Some were even compassionate.

Women not only fantasize about players, they sometimes develop attachments to them, too, even without knowing them.

We were playing the second game of a doubleheader in St. Louis one night, and during the opener I sat in the stands next to this very attractive lady. She said she was a fan, she loved the game, the whole bit; no heavy conversation, just idle chitchat. That was all. Then I said good-bye and left to get ready for our game.

We didn't go back to St. Louis until the following season.

Our first trip there, she was sitting behind the Celtics bench. Our second trip there, she was sitting behind the Celtics bench, with green hair! On our third trip she met me at the airport as soon as our plane arrived and presented me with portraits.

Then I heard that she was leaving her husband.

I'm leaving out nothing in this story.

I talked with that woman exactly three times in my life, twice personally, including once in the bar of the hotel where the team stayed. And then we talked once on the phone when she called my room to say how much she cared for me. I don't remember her exact words, but basically she had this image of me that was driving her nuts.

I wanted no part of this. None. Yet she kept looking up the times of our arrivals, and whenever we pulled into St. Louis she'd be waiting on the ramp with her green hair, just to welcome me to town.

You can imagine how delighted this made Auerbach.

Believe me, it didn't make me much happier.

*   *   *

Women aren't the only ones attracted to the NBA. A lot of gays are drawn to it, too.

That was happening when I played.

Some very prominent men, supposedly avid sports fans, would come into the locker room just to check out the guys. One was a well-known business executive in a road-trip city who happened to be a switch-hitter. That shocked the hell out of me when I found out. We were sitting together at a baseball game and he started to rub my leg, like I was his date! "I'm sorry," I said, "I am *not* in that ballpark," which didn't stop him from taking a shot every once in a while.

And he wasn't the only one.

It all comes with the pro athlete's life-style, and it has many ramifications.

Shy guys, the kind who could never come up with good lines on their own, found they never had to communicate at all. Women came on to them. Why? Because they were famous, they were important, they were *somebody*, and I guess there are gals who feel that making it with a somebody makes them a somebody, too.

Other guys who might have had something lacking in their marriages took pleasure in the time they spent with strangers.

And then there were the guys who saw it as more of an ego boost than anything else. The need for acclaim that drove them to greatness was fortified each time a new partner assured them that they were indeed wonderful.

Back home, meanwhile, wives—well aware of the pitfalls that existed out there in the world—waited for their husbands to return, and upon those reunions I'm sure there was always the urge to wonder aloud, "Have you been screwing around?"

But that was a worry that was rarely addressed,

another of the many accommodations made over the years.

Then one day the traveling's over. He comes home for good, and the drip, drip, drip begins.

Every day. *Every* day.

No more accommodations. No more need for them.

Now the defenses come down, and in seeing each other in a way you've never seen each other before, you find out very quickly if you still have anything in common, or if the truth you've been avoiding all of these years is that the glue of your marriage never set, the diamond was never sufficiently polished, and the time for doing something about it has been lost forever.

It takes two very mature people to emerge from all of this with a healthy marriage intact.

Some couples make it. A lot of couples don't.

° 27 °
Business As Usual

A frustration I often hear voiced today is that sports pages seem to be filled with things other than box scores, features, and final results, which are the things fans enjoy reading.

But these other issues—which I call *freedom issues*—are not going to go away, and unless people take the time to understand them they're going to be turned off by sports.

Besides, if they get to understand them they might even get to enjoy reading about them, just to see who's being a jerk when it comes to matters like free agency.

What's going on in sports is what's going on in every business. I know, fans don't like to think of sports as business; they'd rather focus on the competition. But the owners are in it to make money and the players are in it to make money, and these stories no one likes to read cannot be wished away.

The athlete is the only worker in the country unable to go out and bargain freely for his services the way everyone else does. If you're an engineer who just got out of MIT, a very intelligent, skillful person, comparable in your field to the athlete who's exceptionally gifted in his, you can sift through offers from various companies in deciding where you want to work, where you want to live, and what kind of remuneration you can command by matching one offer against another.

The professional athlete can't do that. He has to enter his job market through a draft.

Most player associations and unions accept the fact that a draft is necessary to maintain competitive balance, allowing poorer teams to pick up better players. It's unquestionably good for the sport, but it also infringes on the freedom of the players, violating antitrust laws.

So players in the NBA have a Sword of Damocles hanging over the heads of management in their threat to take the draft to court, where it's likely they'd prevail.

What they've done instead is use that threat as a bargaining chip, gaining greater monetary rewards for their group as a whole while pushing more and more for a system of free agency.

Free agency means that once a player, having been assigned to a team through the draft, fulfills the obligations of his contract with that team, he ought to be free to go into the marketplace and offer his services to any employer.

Management resists free agency as much as possible, feeling it has an investment in the development of its players' skills and also fearing the best players would end up on the most profitable teams, thereby disturbing the competitive balance the draft was designed to create.

History suggests, however, that teams that aren't astute in handing out big contracts run the risk of boomeranging liabilities. When free agency enjoyed a brief run in the early 1980s, Ted Stepien, then the owner of the Cleveland Cavaliers, indiscriminately lavished "franchise contracts" on players like Scott Wedman, James Edwards, and Otis Birdsong, none of whom were "franchise players." He also squandered all of his first-round picks, so he ended up with a marginal team that had high-priced players and no future.

While he was sending salaries into orbit, lesser teams like Kansas City and Indiana were losing players to predators like New York, Seattle, and Philadelphia. Suddenly, the NBA was faced with five of its members teetering on the brink of bankruptcy, which had everyone in management circles running scared.

The NBA is not a corporation, unlike other pro leagues. It is a *partnership of corporations*. If you and I are partners and I incur a debt I cannot pay, you must pay it. So in this partnership of corporations, a Ted Stepien going down the chute meant his debts would have to have been assumed by the other teams. And there were five teams in peril. As each one went down, its obligations would have been spread around, thereby creating a ripple effect as other teams, inheriting these debts, found themselves in greater jeopardy. A giant corporation like Gulf + Western might have ended up holding the bag for everyone.

What the Players Association did at that point, helping the league avert a crisis, was agree to a restriction of movement called a salary cap, which said players could still go into the marketplace and offer their services, but only to those teams whose payrolls did not exceed prescribed limits.

That's not full freedom, nor were earlier plans that called for teams signing free agents to offer some form of compensation to teams losing them. If an engineer is working for Raytheon, and General Electric comes along to offer him more money, Raytheon doesn't say to General Electric, "Okay, you can have him, but you owe us two technicians in return."

What kind of freedom is that?

The only "freedom" an athlete has is the freedom to quit playing. That's simply not good enough.

So this is the crux of those stories no one likes to read.

The owners are asking, "How can we maintain competitiveness while allowing these guys to have free movement?"

But the players, armed with court decisions that suggest the draft would be declared illegal, have a very strong hand to play when the next round of collective bargaining talks begin.

I doubt they'll play that trump card. The freedom issues are never going to be fully resolved, so what the players will most likely do, as they have in the past, is use the threat of a lawsuit to gain bigger benefits.

I've heard people say, "No one forces the athlete to play. If he doesn't like the league's rules, let him find another job."

It's true. He doesn't have to play. But why should his freedom be restricted just because he happens to be an athlete? Any other business that established rules designed to impede free trade would be struck down immediately. You're not allowed to limit people's freedom to work or buy products in this country. That's what antitrust statutes are for; that's why price-fixing is against the law.

Westinghouse and Raytheon would love to be able to set up a draft to guarantee that engineers from MIT had to work for them or couldn't ply their skills at all. No way. It couldn't be done. It wouldn't be allowed.

Sports is the only business that gets away with this.

The NBA insists it needs these restrictions to remain financially viable. Meanwhile, one of its teams floats a $46 million public stock issue for 40 percent of the franchise, suggesting that the team, the Celtics, is theoretically worth close to $125 million. While players see that happening they also see four expansion teams being admitted after paying initiation fees of $32.5 million each.

Can you blame them for looking at numbers like these, for looking at TV revenues, for looking at the way the NBA is merchandising everything from jackets to paperweights to imitation rings, and saying to the owners, "Hey, boys, what do you say, let's share the pot?"

If I seem sympathetic to the Players Association, it's because I am.

Bob Cousy was its first president. I was its second.

We were like Sam Gompers and John L. Lewis trying to organize coal miners back at the turn of the century. Those coal miners weren't concerned with just monetary benefits and welfare benefits; they were also concerned with working conditions.

So were we.

The first negotiation we tried to hold with the league had to do with a pension plan, but we also wanted full-time trainers. The first five or ten seconds after an injury are often critical; having a qualified person there could shorten your recuperation by days, even weeks. Yet there was often nobody there. By not taking care of us, owners were hurting their own teams. That was one of our first big issues.

We also asked them not to schedule Saturday night games for teams that were going to play televised games on Sunday afternoon. We felt there was no way we could travel all night long after playing and still be able to put on a good performance the following afternoon.

Invariably, the first response of the owners—who related everything we wanted to what it would cost them—was to test our resolve, to test how strongly we felt by telling us, in effect, "Hey, you don't like it? Too bad, pal. These are our rules."

That attitude has always been there, and it led to the most traumatic night of my career, at the 1964

All-Star game in Boston Garden when, under my leadership, players refused to go onto the court when it came time for the opening tap.

I had taken over leadership of the Players Association from Cousy, its founder, in 1958. Cooz had become disenchanted. He'd send out letters asking for dues and maybe a third of the players would respond. So he came to me one day and asked, "Would you be interested in taking my place?" I had been an economics major and I was already in the insurance business, plus I felt the players trusted me, so I told him sure, why not?

I took it seriously. I held organizational meetings with all the visiting teams at the Garden, explaining what we were hoping to accomplish, and I appointed strong members of each team, guys like Bob Pettit, to act as shop stewards. I also began forcefully collecting annual dues, even to the point of going into locker rooms and threatening players who didn't hand over their twenty-five dollars. After a while the word began to spread: "Hey, this goddamn guy is crazy. He means business." I certainly did.

The owners kept promising to meet with us to discuss provisions for a pension plan, then they always found ways to drag their feet. Throughout the summer of 1963 we continued to press them on the issue. Finally, they told us we could present our case at their meeting in New York that November.

Player reps from all over the league showed up at their own expense. Then we all cooled our heels in the hotel, waiting the whole afternoon for the board of governors to invite us upstairs.

The call never came. We were ignored.

So we had a meeting of our own right there. "We've got to take some kind of strong action," I suggested. "My proposal is, if we don't get a pension plan, we don't play the All-Star game. Now I want you guys to go back to your teammates, tell them what happened here, explain our proposed course of action, and let me know if we're all in this together.''

The responses were what I expected. Everyone said, "Let's do it."

In December I went to see Walter Brown, the Celtics owner, a guy we all loved very much. He helped establish the league, and when no one else was willing to risk losing money on the concept of an All-Star game he personally sponsored the first two in 1951 and 1952, even though he was financially strapped. Now the game, an established success, was coming back to his building.

"Walter," I said, "you've been a supporter of the Players Association from the beginning, so I feel I ought to let you know something is going to happen at the All-Star game unless there's action on a pension plan. I'm not sure just what that will be, but I wanted to alert you. I owe you that."

And I did. If all the owners had been like Walter, there wouldn't have been a problem. He was a thoroughly decent, honorable guy. Along with all of the other pressures I was feeling, there was a great reluctance on my part to do anything that would hurt or embarrass him; but, as luck would have it, he was also the All-Star host that year.

A blizzard hit Boston the day of the game. The players were supposed to have been there by noon; we had a meeting scheduled for 3:00 P.M., but because of the storm they kept arriving in dribs and drabs.

As each one came I had him put his signature on a statement of support for the action we were planning. I was protecting my own ass; I didn't want anyone getting cold feet the next day, saying it was all my idea. If that happened, I wanted to be able to pull out a slip of paper and say, "Oh yeah? That's not the tune you were singing yesterday."

I still have those signed statements in my files.

*   *   *

At 5.00 P.M. I went to Commissioner Walter Kennedy's room with Bob Pettit and Larry Fleischer, whom I had hired the year before as executive director of our association, a position he still holds today.

"Walter," I said, "if we don't have a pension plan by game time, you don't have an All-Star game."

"Are you guys crazy? I can't get the owners together now. They're all out having dinner."

"Walter, I'm sorry. But we warned you people something was going to happen."

He was ripping as we left.

When we got to the Garden I had the West team come down to the Celtics locker room where the East team was dressing so we'd all be together, knowing the owners would soon show up, intent on talking their players out of this showdown. Fleischer and I also grabbed Chris the Cop, the old guy who used to guard the Celtics' door, and told him, "Don't let anybody in here unless you clear it with us, okay?"

Chris the Cop, who had to have been seventy, said, "Right."

Bob Short, the Lakers owner, was the first to try.

"Let me in," he said to Chris the Cop. "I want to see Elgin Baylor and Jerry West."

Chris the Cop said, "No one gets in there unless *they* say it's okay."

Short was beside himself. "Well, you march your ass in there right now and tell them I'm out here waiting."

Chris the Cop said, "I will do that, Mr. Short," and in he comes. He walked up to Baylor—I was sitting right next to Elgin when this happened—and said, "Mr. Short wants you and Jerry to come outside right now." Elgin said, "You go tell Bob Short to fuck himself." Chris the Cop shrugged and walked outside with the message.

I'll always remember Elgin for that. It was a very gutsy thing to do.

*   *   *

The game was set for 8:00 P.M.

It was now 7:50 P.M. and all the players were in uniform, but no one had left the room.

Kennedy wanted to talk. We told him he'd have to talk with Fleischer, but he didn't want to acknowledge him as our representative; he said Fleischer had nothing to do with the league. So we talked about that among ourselves and I said, "Guys, I guess what we have to do is make Larry an honorary member of our association. Then if they don't want to talk with him, it means they don't want to talk with us." That's what we did.

Now Kennedy came in. He said there was nothing he could do at that late hour to put a plan together, but that if we'd play the game he would personally pledge to do all he could to see that we got one. Then he left and an argument broke out. Some guys wanted to give him the benefit of the doubt; some wanted to hold out for a firm commitment. Personally, I was inclined to trust Kennedy. I believed him. I just had a good feeling about him. I also thought we had made so much of an issue out of this, with the press watching it all unfold, that there was no way the owners would renege again.

So we played.

The East won, 111–107. I scored 10, but I was in a daze the whole game. I do remember Johnny Kerr saying afterward, "Forget the MVP. The guy who deserves all the awards tonight is Tommy Heinsohn."

That wasn't what I was in it for, but I very much appreciated what he said, especially when I picked up the papers the following morning and saw that Walter Brown had called me "the Number One Heel in sports."

That hurt deeply, because I loved Walter Brown.

I was also upset to see that Wilt Chamberlain told writers, "I never wanted to do this. I was sort of forced into it." Goddamn Wilt! I could have buried him, because I had his signature on one of those slips, along with everyone else's. Granted, he wasn't a player rep; he had come simply as an All-Star. But nobody forced him to sign anything. Nobody broke his arm. Who was going to break Wilt Chamberlain's arm?

I let it pass. I was too wiped out to fight anymore. The bottom line was, we *did* get our pension plan.

And later that spring, at the Celtics' breakup dinner where we celebrated another championship, Walter Brown got up in front of everyone and made a point of thanking me personally for the success we'd enjoyed. Then he and I shook hands. For me, that was the happy ending the story needed.

When I see the money that's being spread around today, along with the magnificent benefits modern players enjoy, I really don't have any sense of envy or regret.

Why should I be upset, when what I'm seeing are the results of things we set out to accomplish a generation ago? We were determined to plant the seeds, knowing full well we wouldn't be around to share in the bountiful harvest. That wasn't going to happen during our careers. The economics just weren't there.

Our stated goal was to set the wheels in motion, that's all.

And we did it. We won our battle.

But the war is a long way from over.

So if you're going to be an informed sports fan, you might as well get used to following it, because it's not going to go away.

° 28 °

Reflections

I think that of all the things I've learned along the way, one of the most important is that everybody can't be a star.

Yet everybody has gifts. Everybody has talents. Everybody has an ego. It's the perfect blending of those gifts, talents, and egos that determines success in basketball, and it's what's missing most in our society today, I think.

We're having a lot of trouble blending our egos.

I watched the Iran-Contra hearings on television, and what I saw was the egos of the Congress fighting the ego of the president. That's what it was to me—egos and images colliding over an issue called Ollie North. *Hey, what's that man's province? What's my province? Which is the most powerful institution in government: mine? or his? or theirs? Who's calling the shots? Who's really in charge here? Damn it, who's running the show?*

Can't we be involved with the substance of people? Do we always have to be caught up in the images?

That's all I saw as I watched that screen from day

to day; one branch of government trying to out-image another branch of government. Both have their place in the scheme of things. Both are important. Yet each was tremendously concerned that the other one might be encroaching. Congress was saying, "The president went too far without our consent," while the president was saying, "This is *my* domain."

Everyone was preoccupied with carving out turf, or so it seemed to me.

But was that what it was all about? Is that what was really important? I saw a president disregard Congress for a reason he felt was legitimate, and I saw Congress try to subvert a president's prerogatives by slipping through the Boland Amendment. They were as devious in their dealings with him as he was in his dealings with them.

What I really saw was a lot of naked ambition.

I'm a basketball guy, so my idea of maximum efficiency is when everyone works together, when everyone pulls in the same direction, when everyone's eyes are fixed on the same goal.

Is that the way our government's percolating?

I don't think so. I think it runs like a team from Albuquerque.

In fact, the more I saw of those hearings, the more I thought what we all need in this country is a good civics lesson.

I retired as a basketball player in 1965.

I was inducted into the Hall of Fame in 1986.

So I lived twenty-one years between those events, years in which I learned a lot about myself.

The Hall of Fame is nice. It will look good in my obituary. But it ceased to be my burning goal many, many years ago, well before I stopped playing. If that were to have been the crowning achievement of my life, the crowning glory, something I needed in order to consider myself a success, I would have been a fool. I would have been a very sick person, emotionally, if I still needed approval for a part of my life that ended in 1965.

The Hall of Fame is an accolade for something that is over, and the best part of that something for me was what I learned, not the praise I received.

Don't misunderstand. It's nice. But I could have lived without it. That would not have killed me. I did not need the Hall of Fame to make my life complete.

The gratification to me was always how I felt about myself, not how other people felt about me.

Some people trade on being a former pro. To some people it's vastly important for the rest of their lives. This may sound callous, but while Ray Nitsche and I were filming a commercial he told me how getting into the Pro Football Hall of Fame had been such a very moving, important experience for him, how much it meant to feel that he was now a permanent part of his sport's history. I listened to him, and I could feel his sincerity, and I was happy for him, but I did not identify with what he was expressing because I did not have those feelings at all.

I'm not singing the old Peggy Lee number "Is That All There Is?" I'm not saying any of this in despair or in a negative way. What I'm saying is that people have to keep evolving in their understanding of themselves, their strengths, and their weaknesses—physically, emotionally, and intellectually.

When you stop doing that you die. You atrophy.

That's one of the good things you learn from sports. You have to keep going; you have to keep taking your shots.

You have to move on.

I started drawing when I was a kid, as a way to amuse myself. At first it was just something to do while the neighborhood kids were banging on the windows, trying to get me to come out so they could beat me up again.

In time I got to like it.

I used to ask my mother to buy me painting supplies, but they were expensive and we weren't a wealthy family. Then one Christmas morning I woke up to find these tiny little tubes of oil paints, a couple of brushes, and a few pieces of canvas board sitting under our tree. I kept thinning the paint with turpentine to make it last as long as possible. When it ran out I went back to pencils and charcoal.

I never had a lesson until I went to college. What skills I have are 90 percent self-taught. It was just something I always could do.

In grammar school the nuns would say, "Tommy, draw us a Christmas scene on the blackboard," so I'd take a Christmas card and copy the picture with colored chalk.

In high school I sketched for the yearbook.

Then one day in college while I was drawing a picture of Joe Welch, the army attorney in the McCarthy hearings—he had a great face that appeared on the cover of *Life*—this priest from the art department saw what I was doing and asked if he could enter it into a college competition. I said sure, and I won third prize. The priest encouraged me to take lessons, to pursue my gift more aggressively, but art was always competing with basketball, and basketball always won.

I sketched all the time on the road while I played, and when I retired I told myself I was finally going to take that priest's advice. So I found a teacher at the DeCordova Museum and studied with him.

Then I went back to the Celtics as coach.

I began taking watercolor kits on the road, painting scenes I liked outside hotel room windows. One day I brought some players to a big men's store in San Francisco. While a couple of them ran in to buy some things I waited in a rented car behind this old building. I became fascinated by its maze of grillwork, fire escapes, and air-conditioning ducts, all of which had contributed their own unique stains to the bricks, which now were multicolored. So I took a few Polaroid shots, and for the next five years I worked on an acrylic of that old building. I've still got it. I've been offered a lot of money for it. The amounts are not important because the picture's not for sale.

Art, to me, is personal.

For years and years I never told anybody I painted. I didn't want anybody to know. I was doing it for my own pleasure, not for anyone else's approbation.

I was coaching the Celtics when I sold my first painting. I'd been sick as a dog, so I checked into the hospital for a few days. On my way there I saw an old doorway that intrigued me, so I took a Polaroid shot, and later, in my hospital room, when I felt stronger, I sat up in bed and did a painting of it. When I got out I brought it to a shop where I left it to be framed, then forgot about it. A few weeks later I returned. "Someone wants to buy your painting," the owner said. I told him I didn't want anyone buying something just because it was painted by the coach of the Celtics. "Tommy," he assured me, "the guy doesn't know who the hell you are. He just likes the painting."

"Okay," I said. "Let him have it."

I was down on Cape Cod once, doing a painting on the beach, when a man came by, liked what he saw, and said, "Turn the other way and paint that house over there—my house—and I'll give you whatever money you want." I said to him, "See you later," and kept painting. I wasn't interested.

That's how Vincent van Gogh was.

If you're going to be an artist, you have to do it for what it means to you. If you're just going to do it to please other people, forget it. You'll never experience the best of whatever it is you can be. That's why I never wanted to do portraits—portraits are painted on command. If anybody tells me, "Paint something *now*," I say, "See you later, baby." I paint when I want to paint. It's my fun. If other people like it, fine. If they don't, that's fine, too.

I've had several one-man shows. I've also participated in shows with other painter-athletes: Rocky Graziano, Jim Bouton, Don Hasselbeck, George Nock, Rosey Grier, Tug McGraw, Toller Cranston. I've been on the "Today Show" with my paintings, too.

Still, it remains personal. The satisfaction I get from painting is like the satisfaction I got from basketball. It's what it means to me that gives it meaning.

The most thrilling day of my life did not take place on a basketball court. It took place in 1970, up in the hills of North Conway, New Hampshire, where I went on a painting workshop. My senses were enraptured by the techniques I learned that week, by my own execution of them, my own decisions. I just knew in my guts at the end of that week that no matter where I turned, no matter where I looked, I could paint whatever I saw.

I *knew* it! What a feeling.

Winston Churchill brought an easel with him wherever he went. He was an excellent painter. I've seen his paintings and read books on them. He was an impressionist who had the ability to have been a master, if it hadn't been for the other things that happened in his life.

By the sheer dint of his personality, he carried the British people through that war. What decisions he made! When they cracked that German code, telling them the Germans were going to bomb Coventry, Churchill was faced with a decision of incomprehensible magnitude. Should he alert Coventry, saving the town but also letting the Germans know the code had been broken, possibly prolonging the war? Or should he say nothing, knowing thousands of lives would be lost?

I think about that whenever I look at his paintings.

Here was an extra-sensitive man, a man with a true love for beauty—you could tell that by the way he talked—taking on the burden of a monstrous decision, which was to sacrifice Coventry in the hope of bringing the war to a speedier end.

What courage.

Winston Churchill has always been one of my heroes.

I like champion prize fighters, too. I admire them. I think they might be the most courageous of all athletes.

I also like the Boston Pops, James Michener, and "Nightline."

And if I were stuck on the proverbial island with a limited choice of entertainment, I'd want three movies: *Boom Town* with Clark Gable, Spencer Tracy, Claudette Colbert, and Hedy Lamar; *Viva Zapata!* with Marlon Brando, Jean Peters, and Anthony Quinn; and my all-time favorite—I'll get up at three in the morning to watch it again—*Captain from Castille* with Cesar Romero, Jean Peters, and Tyrone Power. But if all I could have was music, I'd say give me the music from any of Errol Flynn's movies.

Those were the days when movies entertained you.

I think we're seeing that kind of craftsmanship come back, slowly. I hope so. I'm a fan of movies that elicit real emotions.

I stopped going when it seemed everything became the delivering of messages.

The first movie that really got me upset was *M*A*S*H.*

It was such an obvious political statement, done in a way to ridicule every institution from motherhood to religion to authority without putting back anything good in their places. That's what I abhor: people and systems bent on destroying things with no intention of replacing them with something better.

M*A*S*H was the worst movie I ever saw. Everyone in the theater was laughing like hell except me. I was so angry I got up and walked out.

I've been lucky.

A lot of people have believed in me.

I've dedicated this book to some of them . . . to the ones who cared when it mattered most.

I've learned a lot, partly because I've always been willing to listen. When I was coaching, if some drunk in the balcony yelled down, "Heinsohn! Put in Siegfried!" and it seemed like a good idea, hell, I'd do it. Why not?

But the decision was always mine.

I think I'm still learning . . . about life, about myself.

I certainly hope I am.

If you're a basketball player and you don't work on your game every summer, coming up with new moves, baby, you're in trouble; you've already ceased to grow.

I want to continue to grow. Even now.

So I'm still working on new moves, still looking for new ways to live my life, and still having a hell of a good time at it.

Index